"The Richest and Most Famous Private Chef in the World" Joseph Donon

Gilded Age Dining at Florham with Florence Vanderbilt Twombly

Walter Cummins
Arthur T. Vanderbilt II

Florham Books

"The Richest and Most Famous Private Chef in the World" Joseph Donon: Gilded Age Dining with Florence Vanderbilt Twombly

Prepared by Walter Cummins and Arthur T. Vanderbilt II

Published by Florham Books

First Florham Books Edition 2017

Acknowledgments:

Geoffrey T. Hellman's "The Best of the Best," the Profile of Joseph Donon that appeared in *The New Yorker* (March 10, 1962) is here reprinted with the magazine's permission: Geoffrey T. Hellman / The New Yorker: (c) Conde Nast

Our thanks to Robert DeLage for his permission to use the Joseph Donon memoir and the Donon photographs.

Sources:

Fairleigh Dickinson University digital archieves for Shirley Burden photographs; the Friends of Florham; Les Amis d'Escoffier Society; Robert DeLage; *The New Yorker*; *The New York Times*.

CONTENTS

Chef Donon's Recipes

Joseph Donon's The Classic French Cuisine, *published by Alfred A. Knopf in 1959, was received with great praise, as the master chef made the lessons of his long career with the Twomblys available to thousands of readers. Reviewing the book for The New York Times, Charlotte Turgeon, a specialist on French cooking, noted that reading the work "one has the impression of sitting at the feet of a cher maitre,' who following of percepts of generations of French chefs, is dedicated to making the best of every food. She concludes, "This is not the book for those who want to prepare a meal in fifteen minutes or less, but this is a book for will-be gourmets or those who already have that status and who will delight in knowing how a qualfied wearer of La Toque Blanche gets his results."*

Craig Claiborne, also writing in the Times, credits Donon's decades as chef at the Twomblys during which the cuisine at the many formal dinners was always French. He concludes that "the vast majority" of the dishes described in the book were served the at the Twombly homes and "are as valid and excellent today as they were when Mr. Donon … was a pupil of Escoffier.

The book had five printings and sold 25,000 copies.

Sample recipes follow throughout these pages.

THE CLASSIC
FRENCH
CUISINE

A complete cook book for Americans—the distillation
of a master French chef's lifetime experience
by Joseph Donon
Officier de la Légion d'Honneur

CHEF DONON AND THE TWOMBLYS

The New Yorker called him, "probably the richest and most famous private chef in the world," and there is every reason to believe that Mrs. Twombly's beloved French chef, Joseph Donon, was just that.

Those of us addicted to *Downtown Abbey* know that the staff is always the key to finding out what is happening in a great manor house. We would know very little about life at Florham, about Mrs. Twombly and her daughter, Ruth, were it not for an incredible treasure trove of primary source material – the reminisces of Chef Donon. After the death of Mrs. Twombly in 1952 and Ruth in 1954, Donon retired at the age of 67 with the help of a generous bequest from Mrs. Twombly. In retirement he realized how extraordinary had been what he had witnessed in his career at Florham and with the Twomblys at their homes in New York City and Newport, a way of life gone forever, and set out to record his memories in a draft memoir he dictated to a friend, and in several interviews with *The New Yorker*, including a lengthy profile. "It was an epoch! It was a special time, and the way those houses were run should not be forgotten."

Chef Joseph Donon in the kitchen at Florham

Who was Florence Vanderbilt Twombly? Florence was the favorite granddaughter of Cornelius "Commodore" Vanderbilt, the richest man in the United States who left his fortune to one of his ten children, William, Florence's father, who in eight years doubled the fortune to become the richest man in the world. On November 21, 1877, Florence at the age of twenty-three married twenty-eight-year-old Hamilton Twombly, the young whiz kid who was the financial brains behind her family's New York Central railroad empire, and wealthy in his own right.

Unlike Florence's four brothers and three sisters who seemed to court publicity, this golden

Mansion at Florham

couple disappeared from public view, spending the winter months at their mansion at 684 Fifth Avenue in New York City, the summer at Vinland, their English Tudor manor in Newport next door to The Breakers owned by Florence's oldest brother, and two months each spring and two months each fall at Florham, their 1,200 acre estate in Morris County, New Jersey, where in the 1890s they built a 110-room mansion designed by McKim, Mead & White, with the park-like landscape laid out by the great Frederick Law Olmsted.

The Twomblys had built Florham for their children. As their daughter Ruth remembered, "Florham wasn't for show or vanity. [My Father] decided to put a great deal of his energy and his love of the beautiful into creating an earthly paradise for his four children, especially for his only son, Hamilton, who he hoped would love 'The Farm' as much as he did." But it didn't work out

6

that way when tragedy struck the family. The Twombly's oldest daughter, sixteen-year-old Alice, died of pneumonia on New Year's Day, 1896, on the eve of her society debut. And the Twombly's only son, Hamilton, Jr., drowned in 1906 when he was eighteen and a counselor at a summer camp. By all accounts, Hamilton Twombly never recovered from the death of his son and died a few years later, in 1910. Daughter Florence had married in 1904, so when Chef Donon came to work for the Twomblys in 1917, the household consisted only of Mrs. Twombly, then 63, and her unmarried daughter Ruth, who at the time was 33. And 130 servants to look after the two women and maintain their properties.

But Donon of course had not signed on to cook for two women and their staff. Mrs. Twombly and Ruth lived to entertain, each of them, for instance, holding five major house parties at Florham each spring and five for each of the ladies every fall, with, at each party, 15 to 20 guests and their servants spending several days with them enjoying the bounties of Florham. Additional guests from the Morris County area could swell the numbers at each dinner to 150, with special occasions bringing 600 guests. The ladies arranged smaller luncheons during the week. After the death of Mrs. Twombly in 1952 and Ruth in 1954, a writer for *The New Yorker* asked one long time staff member whether the Twomblys really enjoyed living in so grand a home. "Ah, you needn't worry your head about that. They had fine times here. They were great for parties. What else would a house like that be for but to have fun in?"

Dining Room at Florham

Slight in stature, youthful in appearance when he was hired by Mrs. Twombly in 1917 at the age of 29, Joseph Donon was as tough and savy as they come. When the Italian chef he replaced threatened him, Donon told him that he had fought for France and killed Germans in the War and would not hesitate to kill him. A senior staff member who tried to give him orders in matters pertaining to the kitchen found herself dismissed by Mrs. Twombly the next day. He replaced the kitchen staff and hired his own workers who were intensely loyal to him and stayed with him for decades. When, for instance, Donon wanted fruit from the Orangerie, rather than telling the head gardener he gave his order to the Twomblys' New York City Office, which in turn instructed the gardeners what to bring to him, and when. He had no budget and his expenses were never questioned. His mission was to fulfill Mrs. Twombly's sole request: "The only thing that Mrs. Twombly asked for is that we give her the best of the best." And that he did for 38 years.

Do not picture Chef Donon toiling over hot stoves in the basement of Florham. He had a core staff of five, each with a specialized function, such as: a pastry chef, a cook who prepared all the vegetable dishes, a man in charge of the equipment and machinery. There were always five footmen in the pantry who "wore the court livery just like they had at Buckingham Palace – only in maroon color, the Vanderbilt color." It was Chef Donon's job to oversee and run what was called the "department" which was the core of Florham: dining.

Every day his kitchen prepared meals in two shifts for the staff of 32 who worked inside the mansion and the staff of 80 who worked outside.

"In mid-April I was given the schedule for Florham—so many dinners, so many ladies' luncheons and so many weekend parties."

Every week when Mrs. Twombly was at Florham there were luncheons and dinners for twenty to thirty guests, and every Tuesday Mrs. Twombly would invite two dozen friends from the Morristown area for a ladies luncheon followed by bridge and tea. Lunch was always at 1:30 and "dinner was eight o'clock sharp! We heard that if a guest was late by just five minutes they might not be invited again for months—or years!" Chef Donon would begin to prepare three to four days in advance for the large

Greenhouses at Florham

weekend parties of 125 to 150 guests, which often included midnight suppers that continued on into the small hours of the morning.

As Chef Donon noted: "Mrs. Twombly knew cooking and she knew wines; entertaining was her life and she lived for it. Mrs. Twombly's desire to please her friends was touching."

Serving the "best of the best" began with the best ingredients, almost all available on the 1,200 acres of Florham. From the Florham farm there were Guernsey cows and their own dairy, vegetable gardens "on the hill near Convent Station," greenhouses for all kinds of grapes and melons. "From our greenhouses we could get melons the size of a small beach ball, and grapes the size of my thumb—one bunch would be a foot long! In the orangerie we had every fruit – oranges, lemons, figs—the Ritz Hotel in Paris were not as good as what we had at Florham. We got them fresh in the morning – right to the kitchen door. If I wanted something special or something changed, I would work through our office in New York and they would tell the gardener what to grow." Donon asked for a cave to be built where he grew mushrooms and celery "white as snow and very crisp." Mrs. Twombly had a big greenhouse just for flowers; she really loved orchids—that was her flower. She had them on the table every day. During the second war, we raised steers and lambs on the farm, so we could be sure of our supplies." Before Prohibition, the Florham basement was filled with so much wine and liquor that there were quantities still there after the deaths of Mrs. Twombly and Ruth.

You are seated at

Table

Placesetting for dining at Florham

Chef Donon remembered Mrs. Twombly fondly. "Once a week, at nine o'clock in the morning, Mrs. Twombly would ring for the butler, Frederick Berles, who would come for me, and we would go to see her about our schedules. Every few days though, she would call me to her sitting room to talk about special things, like a birthday cake or something like that. I would sit down with her and she enjoyed that talk—she spoke to me like a mother! She seemed very happy. Occasionally she would ask, 'Are you happy, chef? Would you like a raise?' She had one party after another—that was her life! Oh, she really enjoyed life, her daughter too! Mrs. Twombly was quiet; she ate simple, not too much. She was like a queen. Once a week she would come to the kitchen to see me and said 'good morning' to everyone. She wanted to keep in touch with all the help. She was very nice; very humble for her place. She wanted to say a few words to all my staff."

Running the Florham food service department was nonstop work, but Chef Donon had a day off every week, rested for several hours each afternoon in a bedroom for his use, and took two months' vacation each year. Mrs. Twombly paid for the trips he and his wife took all over Europe and the United States, and when he would submit all his vacation expenses upon his return, he would receive a check for what he had spent.

"Mrs. Twombly was wonderful to me. At Christmas she would give me something special. The office would send me a check, but it was she who would give me the gift—all the time. That last Christmas, in 1951, I remember that I was the only one of the staff she had upstairs. I got in line with all her family and friends – she lined us up! – and she gave me a silver service."

Because of the wise investments of Hamilton Twombly which continued to throw off millions of dollars of income each year, Mrs. Twombly and Ruth were able to have a Gilded Age life into the middle of the twentieth century, as suburbia surrounded Florham and the world changed around them. Those days are long gone, but Chef Donon was right: "It was a special time, and the way those houses were run should not be forgotten."

—Walter Cummins and Arthur T. Vanderbilt II

Chicken à la King

Make a chaud-froid sauce with the cooking broth. Cool the sauce until it is on the point of setting, and coat the chicken with it. To make a thick coating, return the pieces of chicken to the refrigerator to allow the sauce to set and apply a second coat. Decorate each piece of chicken with truffle cut-outs, leaves of tarragon, and bits of pimento, as imagination dictates.

       3 cups sliced leftover poached chicken
       11/2 cups sliced mushrooms
       1 tablespoon shredded green pepper
       1 1/2 cups chicken broth
       4 egg yolks
       3/4 cup cream

Brown the mushrooms in a little clarified butter and put them in a saucepan with the chicken and green pepper. Add the hot chicken broth and simmer for 5 minutes. Beat the egg yolks and cream together, warm the mixture with a little hot broth, and stir it into the chicken and mushroom mixture. Heat well without boiling, adjust the seasoning with salt, pepper, and cayenne, and serve on freshly made buttered toast or in puff-paste shells. Because it is less likely to be dry, poached or boiled chicken rather than roasted chicken should be used for chicken à la King.

Chef Donon's Memoir

THE BEGINNING

I grew up in the village of Vineuil-St. Firmin, about twenty-five miles north of Paris, where my father had a big business. He rented the land, across the road from his farm, from the Château of

Homes in Vineuil-St. Firmin

Chantilly. He had forty cows for his dairy farm and every morning we took them across the road to the gate leading into the fields of the Château. My father had a lot of horses because he was also in the transportation business. It was a big business when I think about it now. My mother, herself, had a business by specializing in many kinds of milk and cream dishes made to order for the local chefs. One was called "coeur 'a la crème" which was a dish made with cream that she formed, in a mold, in the shape of a heart. Many years later I would introduce that dish in America with much success.

Château of Chantilly

I was never interested in my parents' business, instead I admired the gardens at the Chateau and wanted to become a florist—a gardener. At that time my health was poor and my father realized I would never be able to do that type of hard work, so I suppose my parents decided that I should learn a good trade; and because my mother had to cook special dishes for me they decided that the life of a chef would be best. In the neighboring town of Senlis my father knew a chef of good reputation, Antoine Ott, the owner of the   Hotel des Areneas. So it was arranged that I should begin as an apprentice at this hotel. I was thirteen years old but I was big—like sixteen years old.

The owner, Mr. Ott, was formerly the chef at the Château of Chantilly for the Duc d'Aumale. It was a <u>big</u> hotel in those days; over forty rooms. We had three kinds of guests—the men who drove the horses and wagons for their business, like my father,—the tourists—and the society people that the chef knew from his work at the Château. When I started I learned *everything*! I was in the kitchen to do all the kinds of work there was—I even washed the floor (laughs). For the next two and a half years I learned the basics of food preparation and the management of a large kitchen. I also learned how to bottle the wine they would buy in barrels. It was there that I learned what merchandise was good and what was bad, just by the look of it!

We started at 6:30 every morning and worked to past 10:30 at night and during our long daily break, after the dinner service was completed, I enjoyed hearing Mr. Ott talk about his former days as chef at the Château and of the great dinners he had prepared for the Duc d'Aumale who lived there. And so I began to change my mind about wanting to be a gardener. At the hotel we had many English and American guests and one of my duties was to take these tourists to see the Roman arena that was part of the hotel property. I would give these visitors a tour of the ruins and tell them of its history; and they would tip me for that—*one franc!* (laughs)

Hotel de Panisse

After two and a half years at the Hotel it was arranged that I should continue my apprenticeship at the Maison Gervaise in Vincennes, near Paris, where I was to learn everything about pastry. I worked there under a contract for one year and because I was a paying apprentice I learned as much in that one year than the others learned who were serving a three-year apprenticeship. My father was paying the proprietor, Mr. Chaumont, $100 a year, and my contract called for two or three months at every station. At that time I was fifteen years old while the others were just twelve or thirteen. I learned fast and after that year the owner asked me to stay on to assist him in preparing and serving private dinners and he would be paying me $20 a month—and that was good money in those days!

In June, 1905, on Mr. Chaumont's recommendation, I began as third assistant to the chef at the Mexican Embassy for $20 a month. Those homes and embassies were considered <u>tops</u> for a chef in those days. Working in a private house I came in contact, daily, with other chefs at the market place and heard whenever there was an opening in other positions higher than third assistant. In those days you needed the recommendation of your chef in order to advance. So when I heard that a chef Guigou, who worked for a Marquis, was looking for a first assistant experienced in pastry, I asked my chef to speak for me. So, on April 15, 1906, I began in my new position in the home of the Marquis of Panisse Passis at 24 Avenue Marceau in Paris.

Carlton Hotel 1908

Chef Guigou loved opera and would sing his favorite arias to us while in the kitchen. It was there I began to appreciate good music and many years later, in New York, I would know all the famous singers who were part of our French group—I even knew Caruso!

While working in Paris some friends and I would go to the popular opera because we were crazy about that kind of music. They would let us in for just 50 centimes—*nothing*! We went to two theaters, the Ambigue and the Chatelaine, and we even had a part in a play, "Around The World In 80 Days". We were on the stage in the crowd. They needed the extra people and we had the option of being on the stage or up in the balcony to clap. There was a man who would give us a signal to clap; then the audience would clap also. If we were on the stage we had to act like we were speaking, but did not say anything—just to move our mouths.

I was earning $25 a month plus room and board, with two afternoons and evenings off each month. I was doing well as first assistant when something happened that taught me a lesson I never forgot. Chef Guigou sent me to the market to buy some fresh asparagus for a big dinner and on my way I passed a circus and stopped because it was raining. I was soon in a card game and lost the money my chef gave me, plus all my own. After, I found myself walking by the River Seine and I thought that the only way out for me was to jump in (laughs). But I quickly remembered that my uncle lived nearby. He lent me the money I had lost so I could buy the asparagus. Later, I told Chef Guigou and he made me promise never to gamble again—and I never did. (laughs).

I started for the Marquis in April, 1906, and in November we all moved to his big Chateau at Villeneuve-Loubet near Nice on the Mediterranean. The Chateau was built in the twelfth century and the Marquis and his family would live there during the winter months, returning to Paris in April. They had nearly forty people who worked for them at the Chateau. I would go up to the tower to watch the sunrise and could see the island of Corsica on the horizon. On the ramparts of the castle there were orange trees and lemon trees. When I asked the Marquis if I could take some to send to my family he said, "Go take anything you want my boy." He always called me "my boy," I was just a kid—only seventeen!

One day in April, after the family returned to Paris, I was left in Villeneuve-Loubet with the Marquis because, for some reason, he had to remain during those extra two weeks. He told me that the next day be would entertain the great chef Auguste Escoffier—I didn't know it then but it would be the turning point of my life!

I had heard of Escoffier and the idea that I was to cook a meal for him did not make me nervous. But after that luncheon the head-waiter told me that the Marquis wanted to see me and escorted me to the salon where I saw his guest of honor—Escoffier. The Marquis introduced me to this great chef who asked me how old I was. "Seventeen years old, sir," I said, And then he asked me if I would like to work for him at the Carlton Hotel, in London.

It seems that the Marquis arranged this for me and soon I was dreaming about going to London to work for Mr. Escoffier! I arrived there May 7, 1907.

At that time the Carlton was the most popular hotel in England and its Ritz Restaurant, managed by Escoffier, was the most famous in Europe. I arrived at the Carlton with my little suitcases but the doorman would not let me in. My English was very poor and he could not understand that I was coming to see Mr. Escoffier (laughs). Well, one of the kitchen staff passed by and I guess he understood me, because he was also French, and brought me around to the kitchen entrance and told me to wait. In a few minutes a man came out, took my suitcases and there I was, in Mr. Escoffier's office. He asked me, "Who are you? Where are you coming from?" I explained that I worked for the Marquis, in Villeneuve-Loubet, and that I was invited to work at the Carlton. He looked at me and then he seemed to remember and smiled (laughs). He hired me for seven shillings a week and arranged for me to share an apartment with two others from the kitchen. I worked on the preparation of meals and moved from station to station; again, learning in a few months what would take years if I had to

Auguste Escoffier

wait for advancement from one station to another. There were seventy men working in the kitchen at the hotel. Mr. Escoffier was watching me and he saw that I could take the place of anyone there—because of my experience.

One day he asked me if I would work for a very rich family, Danish, who had a big business in India—the Hansen family. In those days England had lots of wealth from India. Well, their chef broke his leg and they needed another chef right away to take his place. Because I had experience in private houses he asked me to work for them. After a few weeks they asked me to stay with them and I asked, "What about the other chef?" They said, "Don't worry about him—he's gone!" Well, when I found out that it was all right with Mr. Escoffier I stayed for almost six months, and after that they asked me to go to India with them. I told them that I had to do my military service soon and, anyway, I still worked for Mr. Escoffier, so I must ask him. I returned to the Carlton but he arranged for me to work at the new Royal Hotel that was opening in Evian, in France, for the summer. After that he told me to return home to do my two years of military service, and after being discharged I was to come back to London to work for him again.

In September, 1909, I entered the French Army and was stationed at the Fort of Montmorency. In those days there were forts all around Paris. We had to go up that Mont in a special train and our fort was under the ground. We lived there, underground, and we had our kitchen there too. At that time the Army was just renovating their kitchens and my assignment was to establish a system to buy food for all the forts around Paris. I went shopping with four or five men and a truck, and I carried a big book with me, that they gave me, to make my purchases and have the proprietors sign it. I was on a budget and we were allowed only so much for each man in the battalion of Paris. I remember we were allowed 10¢ each man for fresh meat, and 10¢ each for preserved meat a day. The big markets in Paris would open early in the morning and by eight o'clock all the hotels and restaurants, and all the chefs, would have their purchases made. So after eight o'clock everything was wholesale, and I would always buy at the wholesale prices. I enjoyed that work for the Army and my time went by fast.

Homard à l'Américaine
(Lobster à l'Américaine)

Cut up the live lobsters as follows: sever the claws, cut the tails into sections, split the bodies in half lengthwise, and remove and discharge the little bag near the head. Reserve the tomalley, or green liver, of the lobster, and the coral, or eggs; these will be used for finishing the sauce. Season the lobster with salt and pepper and toss the pieces in a few tablespoons of hot olive oil over high heat until the meat has stiffened and the shells are red. Pour off and discard the olive oil. Sprinkle the lobster with shallots and the garlic, finely chopped and simmer for a few minutes, covered. Add ½ cup cognac, cover the pan, and simmer for 5 minutes. Add the dry white wine, the tomatoes, seeded and chopped, and the chopped herbs. Cover the pan and set it in a moderate oven for 20 minutes. Transfer the lobster to a heatproof serving platter. Reduce the sauce in the pan to one third its original volume and add to it the reserved liver and coral and a little sweet butter. Cook for a minute or two, swirl in 1 tablespoon sweet butter, and adjust the seasoning with salt, pepper, and cayenne. Pour the sauce over the lobster, sprinkle with ½ cup heated cognac, set the spirit ablaze, and serve flaming. Serves 10.

TO AMERICA—ON THE "TITANIC"

After my service I went back to the Carlton Hotel where I resumed my work and one night, in April, 1912, I was in charge of a big dinner for a wealthy American, Henry Clay Frick.

Young Joseph Donon

Afterwards, before we left, Mr. Frick's personal secretary, Mr. Holroyd, came to the kitchen to talk to the executive chef who was in charge that evening. They came over to me and I was introduced to Mr. Holroyd who gave me a $20 gold piece in appreciation of the dinner that Mr. Frick enjoyed -- I thought he was giving me a medal because I had never seen such a gold piece before! (laughs). I was surprised when he asked me if I would like to come to America as Mr. Frick's chef. Well, I went to talk to Mr. Escoffier about it and he made the arrangements for me, also giving me letters of recommendation for the Ritz Hotels in New York and Philadelphia if I found I did not like it with Mr. Frick. It was arranged that I would be paid a salary of $150 a month, plus $150 for my personal expenses, also room and board. I was given a second-class passage ticket on the "Titanic", and was told to be ready to sail on April 10, 1912.

In those days you could not enter the United States as a servant employed by a wealthy person; you had to come on your own. They only required you to have at least $250, so you would not be a burden on your new country. Mr. Frick paid my passage but I had to pass the hat around the Carlton kitchen to raise that money (laughs). Just before I was to leave I received word that Mrs. Frick had injured her ankle in Southampton on her way to the ship and that the family was returning to London until she was better. You know, that saved our lives!

I did leave England, on May 3rd, on the German ship "Amerika", with the Frick family, and we passed the wreckage of the "Titanic" on our way. The kitchen and dining rooms were under the management of the Ritz-Carlton, and I spent some of my time in the kitchen because I knew the chefs working there.

We landed at Hoboken, New Jersey, and after passing through immigration I was all alone on my own and I realized I did not have Mr. Frick's address! When I explained to the cabdriver that

Frick Home at 640 Fifth Avenue

my employer was a rich man he took me up Fifth Avenue where we stopped every block to ask where Mr. Frick was living. But then, on the corner of 51st Street, and right across from the Frick house at 640 Fifth Avenue, was Mr. Frick's secretary, Mr. Holroyd, looking for me!

That evening Mr. Holroyd and I went by train to Prides Crossing, Massachusetts, where the Fricks had a big summer home called Eagle Rock. It was right on the coast; the North Shore of Boston. On one side of the road was the stable and garage and a building that made the electricity for the whole estate, so they would not have to rely on the town for power. There was also a big garden for vegetables and a special line for the family's private railroad car. On the other side was the house on top of a hill, and from the house you could see the harbor at Marblehead. It was a *big* house; pretty near as big as The Breakers, with over thirty servants. I had two assistants and a handyman in my department. I was only twenty-three years old and I was the first Escoffier-trained chef to work in a private house in America. At that time I had no plans for my future and I never knew that I would be living in America all my life. Before I left Mr. Escoffier, he told me that I would have to show the Americans how to run their kitchens and that I should stay calm and run my department without interference. He also told me not to be surprised at anything I might see in America (laughs). He was right because when I first went into that kitchen I saw only a stove and a few pans—that was all. Before me there had been a woman cook and nothing was organized—but I was sure of myself, I always was, and I put things under control.

Prides Crossing

Mr. Frick was a kind man; warm and friendly. He came up from *nothings*! He was German-Swiss. He was very smart but the unions were against him because he didn't believe in what was behind them. He was probably the richest man in America at that time; no question about it—he was worth a hundred million! He owned the coke and you must have that to make steel. Mr. Frick needed the railroads; that was the Vanderbilts—and the railroads needed his business. Frick made Carnegie because Carnegie needed the coke for his steel mills. Mr. Frick was a good friend of the man (Edward J. Berwind) who owned The Elms here in Newport. I don't know why he never built here because he knew lots of people from Newport. They were all big businessmen—they made America what it is today.

At Prides Crossing Frick had a special railroad track built near the side of the house, where he kept his private car; it was just fifty yards from the house. He kept two colored men on board, one was the cook; the other was a waiter. Their quarters were next to the kitchen and he went all over the country in it. He had two valets; one white, who took care of his clothes. The other was a colored man, Percy, who did the errands and went all over on business for Mr. Frick—he was the trusted man of the family. Percy was my buddy there. When I needed some special supplies he would go to the town of Beverly on his motorcycle for me.

Mrs. Frick and her daughter, Miss Helen Frick, ran the house. They were both very natural people—shy. Mr. Frick didn't bother with the house; he was the businessman. Miss Frick would always come into the kitchen to watch me work. She would speak to me in French because she went to school in France and could speak the language perfectly. She would come to fix the menu for the day and often she would ask me to make turtle soup because her father loved that. One day she said they would like Boston

Henry Clay and Adelaide Frick

Baked Beans. She told me the family liked that and would like to have it served once in a while. Well, I was just in America two weeks and I had to find out about all the meats and supplies here because it was different from what I knew in France and in England. I asked, "What is that?" She said it was made with beans and pork! I knew that in France we have a dish with those ingredients so I said, "All right, I know that." Well, the next morning she came in with a big smile and told me that the family liked the dish I made, but wondered what kind of Boston Baked Beans they were eating (laughs). She told me it should be made with molasses, and we both laughed about it! She was always very friendly and personal; a very natural girl.

Her brother, Childs Frick, was an explorer and when I started for the family he had just returned to the house from Africa and brought back a pygmy as a *valet*! He would bring home many people from all over the world and ask me to cook all kinds of foods associated with the places those people came from. And I had to cook, for his new valet, some special dishes of vegetable roots. There was a big garden on the property, quite a few acres, where they had fruit trees. I would make preserves from the peaches and Mrs. Frick would have that for breakfast every day.

The family had lots of dinner parties and I heard that Mrs. Frick liked to say that I worked for Escoffier at the Carlton Hotel in London. When I needed extra help a good chef from Boston would come up to work for me. It was at Eagle Rock that I first met Archer Gibson, who was the best organist in America. He would come for the weekend to play during the dinner. When he found out that I liked opera he would ask me what I would like to hear, and put those pieces into his program. You could hear the organ even from the kitchen. We became good friends and many years later we would meet again.

In-October Mr. Frick returned to his house in New York and a few days later Mrs. Frick and Miss Frick left Prides Crossing—I was left alone and no one told me to come to New York. I had a phone call from one of my staff and they said that Mr. Holroyd changed all the help in my

Archer Gibson

department! Holroyd was Mr. Frick's secretary for twenty years and he ran the houses for him. I sent a wire to Mr. Frick to say that I was still in Prides and if he did not want me anymore to tell me officially, and send me a recommendation so I can carry on my work. Well, I had a call on the phone and it was Mr. Frick who asked me if I still wanted to work for him, and I said, *"Of course!"*— he told me to come back to New York right away and see him. When I arrived there he told me that from then on I would deal directly with his office in Pittsburgh. He said that I knew my business and I did not have to go through Mr. Holroyd again. You know, after that, Holroyd never had the same duties anymore—after that Mr. Frick never gave him much to do.

The Fricks were living at 640 Fifth Avenue; a big house that had been built for William Henry Vanderbilt—the *great* businessman. Just next door was the home of Mr. Vanderbilt's daughter, Mrs. Sloane (later Mrs. Henry White); I could look through our kitchen windows to see into the other kitchen across the yard. I knew the chef there very well and even went to help out when Mrs. Sloane was having a big party. When her brother, William Vanderbilt, came from Paris every winter, to stay for two or three months at his home on the next corner (660 Fifth Avenue), I would also go there to help his chef who I knew when I worked at the Mexican Embassy in Paris. He asked me how I could now be a chef in "such a house" in America when I was only an assistant just a few years before! Back in Paris I had heard about the Vanderbilt family but it did not mean anything

Clayton

to me then—now, I found myself working in their houses. When the Fricks were giving a large party, and I would need some help in my department, I could get the extra people through my introduction, from Mr. Escoffier, to the chefs at the Ritz-Carlton Hotel in New York -some of them worked with me in London. Many years later, after Escoffier visited New York, we started a chef's organization that is still going strong today!

The Fricks lived in east Pittsburgh, about six weeks a year, always around Christmas time. Their house was called "Clayton"; a big house made of brick, and in the back were large greenhouses. The gardener, a Mr. Fraser, took me all over Pittsburgh because I was new and didn't know anyone, and I needed someone to show me around. He took me to the store where Frick worked as a clerk when he was a young man. Mr. Frick set up an appointment for me to visit the Old Overholt Brewery, that he owned, and taste the whiskey they made there. I didn't know anything about whiskey—I was just a kid! They made me taste it, and I told them I liked brandy better than that (laughs). I remember that in Pittsburgh there was lots of gas underground and places where they burned it all day, so that when they had snow it was covered with black ash in a few hours.

The next spring I was glad to be back in Prides Crossing where I had friends who worked for the Frederick Prince family in the next town; Hamilton, Massachusetts. The Prince house was—like a *castle*! All the staff were French. When I heard that there was a group from the other side (France) I visited there. Mr. Prince used to go to Pau, for the fox hunting, every season, and he brought his staff back to America with him. His wife used to bring her own sheets and pillows with her—the whole bed! In the village of Prides Crossing I met a French family; the father, Victor Blaudin, had a pharmacy. I would go there after work to spend the evening, and I became engaged to his younger daughter, Charlotte, who worked as a secretary in Boston. We planned to be married the next winter, on January 11th, 1914. I saw Miss Frick and told her that I was going to take a couple of days off, then, to get married, and she said, "What! No honeymoon?" I didn't want to leave the house any longer than that because my staff would not be able to run things as well without me. I did arrange for a chef to take my place but when I returned Mr. Frick told me, "Do you know what he served us for breakfast? Sardines and rice! I don't want him here anymore."

Donons' wedding photograph

During this time I was asked to plan the service area of Mr. Frick's new house on Fifth Avenue and East 70th Street. I worked with the architects, Carrere and Hastings, on the kitchen and the service area; the work was done by Duparquet, Huot and Moneuse Company, the French firm. They were the best company for that and they did all the houses there and in Newport—I worked very close with Huot on the design of that kitchen. As it happened I would never work there, because of the war, but I watched them build the new house stone by stone. Later, when Mr. Frick died, and I was working for Mrs. Twombly on the next corner, they made the house into the Frick museum.

Frick Home on Fifth Avenue and E. 70th Street in 1915, now the Frick Museum

In August, 1914, when I heard the news about the start of the war, I left Prides Crossing the next day to check at the French Consulate in New York because I was still a French citizen and was in the reserve army. At the Consulate they told me there were two boats about to leave, and gave me a <u>pass,</u> so I can make the trip for nothing. But I paid for a cabin because we had 1800 men going on my boat and I didn't know how long before I would sleep in a bed again, and I wanted to be sure I had a bed on that boat (laughs).

I had orders to leave on the "S. S. Rochambeau", on August 12th, and before I returned to Prides Crossing to put my business in order I went down to Times Square where the newspapers put up the bulletin of the German victory of the day before, and everybody cheered. At that time the people expected that the Germans would win in a few days because Germany was much stronger than France. But later, when they saw what the Germans did, the country turned to the French side.

When I returned to Prides to tell Mr. Frick when I was leaving I found that all his English help, the footmen, were also leaving right away. That's how it was—we wanted to get back to help our countries. We were in his study, at Prides Crossing, and he wished me good luck but said he believed the war would be over before I could get back. He was not even mad when I told him I was leaving *so fast*. It left him without any help because all the others were English, and they were leaving too. I don't know how he managed without us. Before I left the newspapers were full of stories about me; they called me, "the highest paid chef in the country." They

Donon recuperating from his wound

26

thought I was crazy to go back to France!

As our boats were leaving New York harbor we were all on deck and we passed boats full of Germans who were trying to get back to their own country—like us. They couldn't leave because the English warships, that were waiting to go along with us, were off the coast. As we passed those Germans we made all kinds of noise—and *they* also made all kinds of noise! At that time we thought we had to make that demonstration but now, when I think back to that day, we were foolish—but we had to do it.

They sent my regiment to the Front right away and I was all right until February 13, 1916, when I was wounded, when a piece of a shell hit my shoulder. It was a Sunday and I remember that day because it rained like the devil! The Germans were supposed to make the *big push* that day and they began by shelling everything. I was wounded at 6:30 in the morning. As it worked out the Germans could not move because everything was mud. You know, I was not supposed to be there; I had my pass for furlough in my pocket. My officer said to me, "Why don't you take your pass and go."; but I wanted to stay because my friends were there. After I was wounded I was sent to a hospital in France, and later came back to America in August. At that time, after a battle, we would go out to pick up our wounded and the Germans would also be there under the truce, and we exchanged our wounded and exchanged tobacco. We talked to them because we knew a few words of German or English, and they knew some words in English and French. When I think of it today, it seems foolish that we could *stop* the war and go talk to them like that, and after we had our wounded we started to shoot again!

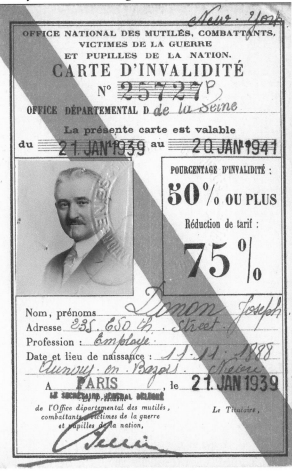

Donon's Carte d'Invalidité

Well, when I arrived back in America I was the first one to return and I found that America changed its mind about the war. Even Mr. Frick was in charge of the committee to welcome Marshal Joffre at the new house on Fifth Avenue. Joffre was the hero of the big battle of the Marne, and he came to America to help raise money for the Liberty Loan.

Chef Louis Diat

I returned to Prides Crossing because my wife was living there with her parents at the time. I worked for Mr. Frick for one month but I was not well and the staff was not organized. My shoulder was bad and I spoke to three doctors about what they could do to fix. me up; I couldn't use my left arm. Those doctors examined me and wanted me to sign a paper that said it was all right to operate and that Mr. Frick would pay bill! Imagine that! They wanted to soak him with a big bill! I told them that Mr. Frick did not owe me anything. I owe him, because he brought me to America—he gave me the opportunity to come here. Well, there was a Dr. Johnson who knew my wife's parents and he came to see me and he told me he would fix me up and would not charge me -I would only have to pay for the hospital room. At that time I did not know how long I would be out of work so I told him, "All right, go ahead."

I went to the Beverly Hospital for the operation where that doctor took one of my ribs to build me a new shoulder. That was in September, 1916, and I did not work again until that December when my wife and I moved to New York so I could follow my career. I had to try to work somewhere until I would see if I can manage again on my own. So I arranged to work for the chef who ran the kitchen at the Ritz-Carlton Hotel in New York—chef Louis Diat. I worked with him in London, and the New York Carlton was *tops* in those days. He told me to take my time and get acquainted with the kitchens again because I had not worked for two and a half years. Mr. Huot, from the firm that made all the kitchen equipment, from my plans, for Frick's new house, came to see me and he gave me a check for $150 to help me out, because I was a 'Frenchman who was wounded and came back. Believe me, I could use that check at the time—oh boy!

Mr. Frick gave me this letter of introduction, dated February 16, 1917....

"To Whom it may concern -
Joseph Donon was in our employ for three years as chef, and left to go to the

28

war between France and Germany.

He gave us entire satisfaction and we can highly recommend him.

H. C. Frick"

"Please come—to see Mrs. Twombly"

One evening, in March, 1917, my wife and I were in our apartment on 110th Street in New York when we heard a knock, and I said to look before she opened the door. She said it was a man in a chauffeur's uniform who held a letter from Miss Twombly; it was her personal chauffeur. The letter read…

"March 17th

Joseph Donon

Dear Sir,

I hear from Mr. Frick that you are looking for a position. Will you kindly meet me at 5 East 73rd St.', on Monday morning next, the 19th, at 11:30 o'clock.

Truly

Ruth Twombly"

Miss Twombly interviewed me at her sister's (Mrs. William Burden's) house on 73rd Street. She saw that I was young and asked if I could run my department! It was true, I looked *young* then and I kept my moustache to make me look older! At that time servants had to be clean-shaven—the family wanted that. I kept mine until I had an accident one day and I cut it off—and people looked at me and they didn't know me (laughs). Well, Miss Twombly asked me, "Are you sure you can manage it?" I told her that I had fifteen years of training for that and I managed well for Mr. Frick. She understood that I could not do any heavy work, because of my shoulder, and she said it was all right because they wanted someone to run the department—to *manage* it—that I could hire whatever help I needed. She told me I would hear from her soon and the next day I received this note,….

Ruth Twombly

"Chef:

Will you please come to 684 Fifth Avenue on Wednesday morning next, the 21st at 9:30 to see Mrs. Twombly.

Truly
Ruth Twombly"

The Twombly house was on the corner of Fifth Avenue and West 54th Street; it occupied

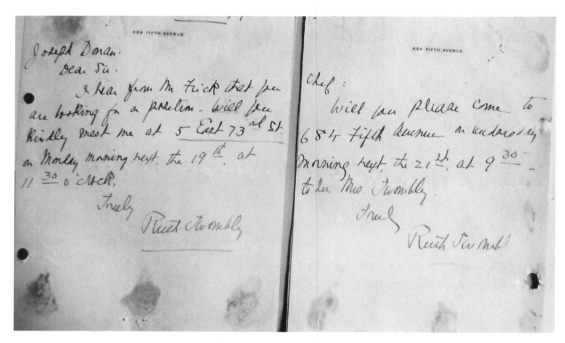

Ruth Twombly's letter to Joseph Donon

almost half the block. Next door was the house of Mrs. Webb, one of Mrs. Twombly's sisters, and behind was the house of John D. Rockefeller. She asked me to start on Monday, April 2nd; the 1st was Easter Sunday that year. She was very considerate because she knew I could not get any supplies that day, so she said to start Monday at breakfast time. I understood that the kitchen was fully equipped, so I would bring my own personal equipment and a truckload of supplies.

I found out later that Mr. Frick knew Mrs. Twombly well and was having dinner at her house, and they spoke about the food because Mrs. Twombly wasn't satisfied with her chef at that time. Frick told her about me—I suppose he said that I was the first one to return to America but he didn't know if I could manage with my arm. He gave me a good recommendation. Later, he would give me my first 'tip', to buy U. S. Steel, through his chauffeur, George, who I knew well.

The chef who was then working for Mrs. Twombly was an Italian; a fine chef but he could not manage his department because he was not trained for that—he was not there very long. When he heard he had been replaced he was mad like the devil. Before he left he threw everything into the trash; he did not leave me even one egg -he just left the stove! Later, the people who were there before me said that if I had come to the kitchen, to introduce myself, before I started, that he would throw me out! You know, the first day I worked for the Twomblys the other chef, the Italian, came back to see me—they called me to the door and he wanted to start a fight with me: I told him, "Listen, it wasn't too long ago I was killing Germans and I can finish you too – quick!" He turned around and he ran! (laughs). Mrs. Twombly wanted French cuisine exclusively. Before the Italian chef there was a French chef who worked for the family for fifteen years—an older man who ran things in the old way. When I arrived the people who worked in the kitchen didn't care how things were run anymore—so I started over fresh. I had it tough for a while because I was still new there.

Before I came to America, Escoffier told me to keep full control of my department because people will try to take that away from me—it was true when I worked for Frick, and I found the same when I started for the Twomblys. The housekeeper in New York came to see me and said that I must come to her for everything, and that I must do my marketing at a certain store. She had her visitors come to the house and it made lots of work for the kitchen—almost as much as I had for the family! I told her I did not understand what she wanted, and to put it in writing. She was foolish to do that because I sent a note to Mrs. Twombly to ask who I was working for, "the housekeeper, or you?" When she asked me to explain what I meant I told her I wanted to know, to be sure of my position, as I understood that I was to have full control of my department. I showed her that note, and she could not believe that that went on in her house. You know, the next day the housekeeper was gone—just like that! Later, at the New Jersey house, I had trouble with the watchman. He was to supply me with the coal I used for the stoves; every morning he was to leave me enough to have everything ready for breakfast. I went in one morning and I found there was no coal, and when I asked him he told me that I had already used *enough* for the week! I called up the office in New York and they said that he told them I was using *too much* coal! I said, "You mean to tell me that the *watchman* is to decide how much I am to use?" I guess that they saw my position because I never had trouble after that.

And then I found that the suppliers tried to bribe me for the business. One put a $50 bill in my pocket, and I asked him why he did that. He said that he appreciated the business from the Twomblys, and it was a gift to show his appreciations! I gave it back to him and told him I would choose my suppliers by the quality of the merchandise, and by the price. I tried all the dealers, and some put up their price by as much as 50% when they found I was buying for Mrs. Twombly. That first day I started for the family a truck full of provisions came to the house—I didn't order

**Florence Vanderbilt Twombly
John Singer Sargent portrait**

it. The man told me he had a "standing order" so I accepted it that day and later I went to see Miss Twombly and she didn't know anything about it—so I cancelled the order for the next day. Do you know what happened? Those dealers wrote to Mrs. Twombly and complained about me! When she showed me those letters and I explained to her that to get the quality she wanted, and not be taken advantage of, I should have control over what I bought and I should be the one to decide what to buy and where to buy it—if I wanted to make a change I should be able to do it. I should be free to pay more than usual sometimes, in order to get the best of the best—to get the results she wanted. If I am to have someone tell me *where* I am to buy the supplies that I would leave—get somebody else. Mrs. Twombly agreed with me. She said that is what she wanted, and that it was all right with her. She told me, "You are right chef—carry on." Later I heard from Miss Twombly's maid, Claire, that they told her, "We like our chef. He is terrific!"

You know, when I began to work for the family there were already people there who started before me. I was asked to organize things as they should be done and was given "carte-blanche". America was still at war in 1917 and we had a hard time to get some supplies. In the New York house I would find some things *missing*: When I left at night I knew we had so much sugar or tea or coffee—the next morning I found some gone. I asked the watchman if he knew who might be taking it—I trusted him. He said that he did not see anyone there but he always made his route the same time every night, and everybody in the house knew where he was at a *certain* time. They knew when he was on the third floor or in the kitchen; so he told me he would change his schedule. We found out who was taking it—it was a girl who worked for the family for years! I had just started then and I didn't want any trouble. I didn't want to accuse her because I heard that she had the *trust* of the family, and if I accused her she would have to deny it to my face. So I put up a metal gate, like an accordion, at the door to the kitchen, to stop anyone from taking anything. I also had a cupboard made with a compartment for each of the people who

Florham

worked in the house; each compartment had a number and a lock, and each person had their key. Everyone who worked there could take whatever they needed from the kitchen supplies, for their own use. They had what they wanted when they wanted it. After that we never had any trouble again. Of course the servants talked among themselves, and Miss Twombly's maid told her about my changes right away. Miss Twombly understood everything and the next day she met me with a smile and said, "Well chef, I hear that you made some changes!" (laughs).

During that first year I worked for the Twomblys I had to learn the tastes and the schedules of the family, and I made plans to update the kitchens in all three of their houses. Mrs. Twombly and her daughter lived in New York from late November until the end of April when they would move to their country home at Convent Station, New Jersey, that was called "Florham"—a combination of the first names of Mrs. Twombly and her husband, Florence and Hamilton. In mid-April I was given the schedule for Florham – so many dinners, so many ladies' luncheons, and so many weekend parties for the months of May and June. Florham was a big house, about a hundred rooms—like a palace on the inside. You know, America is a big country and those people built *big*! The house was planned for just those weekends; it was the most important part of the week for them and we prepared all week to entertain. They owned about a thousand acres—half of the property was like a park around the house and the other half, across the road, was used as a farm.

Florham Farm

They raised Guernsey cows and had their own dairy right there but the vegetable gardens were on the Florham side, on the hill near Convent Station, and there we had greenhouses for all kinds of grapes and melons. I asked them to build me a cave where we could grow mushrooms and other special things. I had them grow celery there—it was about half the size you see in the market now, but it was white as snow and very crisp. All of Mrs. Twombly's guests loved it and asked her where she bought it. They couldn't believe that we grew it right there on the property.

Florham was like a city. We had our own water and made our own electricity. The electric plant was connected to the house by a tunnel and I could use that tunnel when I went to talk to the electrician about matters in the house. Only the gas came from the outside—piped in from Madison. There were eighty men who worked in the gardens and over at the farm. I know because I went to see the head

A Vanderbilt-Twombly family Rolls Royce

gardener, Mr. Hope, about something one day and I saw a list of all those who were working on the grounds. In those days the men really worked—today they would just want to pass the time (laughs).

Thirty-two people worked in the house alone—I had five people in the kitchen and the butler had five waiters in the pantry. There was a plumber, a mason, a painter, a carpenter, and a man who worked in the water pump-house and made the blocks of ice we used in the kitchen. There were three men in the stables, and all the chauffeurs, and when we sent things to the kitchen in their building we packed them in ice, so we used a lot. There were watchmen who would have to use the turn-key clocks all over the place; but we had trouble there, one big weekend, when somebody came into the house. On those big weekends there were people all over the house and the gardens. So one time Miss Twombly's maid, Claire, was on the bedroom floor and she saw a man there and she knew he could not be a guest by the way he was dressed. She kept her head and telephoned for the police; we could hear the siren coming all the way from Madison. That man must have heard it too because he ran from the house. They never caught him but I remember some people saying that they saw a man running away.

When I started for the Twomblys the estate office in New York asked me how many people I served in the servants' dining room; and when I told them they asked me to tell them who I served.

Well, I didn't know them so I asked the headwaiter to pass a piece of paper, for a list, and have everybody sign their name. The office asked me to keep a list of all meals I served and tell them every month. Just for the servants' dining room we had two services because some of the help worked in the kitchen and we had to eat at different times. Sometimes we would have twenty or twenty-five at the first service, and then more for the second service. Some of the help, like Mrs. Twombly's maid, and Miss Twombly's maid, were served in their own dining room.

Table linen and place settings at Florham

We had a small kitchen, for the outside help, located near the side entrance to Florham, on the road to Madison. The main kitchen, in the house, was as big as the kitchen at The Breakers; but when I remodeled everything I put on an addition of three special rooms to keep the provisions—each a special temperature. One for the meat—one for the fish, where we used only ice to keep them fresh—and one room, at forty degrees, for the vegetables. That room for vegetables had wire baskets on the walls. We put the vegetables in there to have the air circulate around them -it keeps them fresh until we are ready to use what we need. Mrs. Twombly told me that she only enjoyed vegetables at home. Even those at the Ritz Hotel in Paris were not as good as what we had at Florham (laughs). Well, we had our own garden there and we got them fresh in the morning—right to the kitchen door. I made a list of every vegetable that could grow in this climate. If I wanted something special, or something changed, I would work through our office in New York, and they would tell the gardener what to grow. That was the only way I could be sure to get what I wanted and the gardeners, Mr. Hope and Mr. Allen, would laugh and tell me, "Chef, are you still in the army? We call you the 'Colonel', because *you* give the orders!" (laughs). That is how they would joke with me.

Upstairs, over the main kitchen, were rooms for all the women servants. At one side of the kitchen yard was the laundry, and just outside the yard was an addition for all the men who worked in the house. On the first floor of this wing were the sitting rooms and recreation rooms for the men, and above were the bedrooms; each room had a sink, a stone bowl with faucets and a mirror on top. The headwaiter had a room there, and there were rooms for all the valets. I had a room there, with my own bathroom, if I wanted to use it, but in those days I wanted to live off the estate because I wanted to be free and not bother with the help in the other departments—like we were taught in France. I told the people who worked in my department to keep by themselves and not mix with the others. I saw to it that they were well paid to live outside the house in New York, but at Florham, and at Vinland, they lived in the house. My wife and I rented a floor from a couple, the Ryans, who lived on Beech Avenue, just fifteen minutes walk from Florham; but I heard that the Twomblys wanted to build a house for me there. You know, it's funny, but Miss Twombly liked to talk to one of the watchmen at Florham. She liked him—he was an Irishman and he used to talk to everybody, so he would tell her what everyone said. One day he told me that the Twomblys wanted to build me a house because everybody else lived there; and there were quite a few houses on the property for the others. I told him that all the time I worked I always lived outside, because I wanted to be independent—no, I said I would not live at Florham. Well, he told Miss Twombly— oh, she didn't like that; (laughs). She said, "Oh, so he wants to be independent?! Well, it's all right—I like him anyway." He told me that later—oh boy!

Vinland

In Newport, at Vinland, I had my own room but I always lived outside. They had one floor for the women there; one for the men. The kitchen was on the first floor with all the windows facing the ocean. I always liked it there because it was a good spot—we could look out and see the water and the flowers near the house. In those days the Cliff Walk was the best thing in Newport; they

37

had flowers from one end to the other! I would see Mrs. Twombly's grandson, Shirley Burden, watching the gardeners there—he *loved* to ride on the mowing machine when they cut the grass.

My room was upstairs and I had windows all around. I used it for my office and rest room; I had a bathroom and a shower. I needed that because I always wore white—so I changed a few times a day. In the afternoon I would rest there for two hours, and I would also use the rooms early in the mornings that I went fishing. Under the kitchen we had rooms for storage; for the cooking wines, and for the provisions that came in from Florham every day. The room where we kept the vegetables had the same kind of wire baskets on the sides that we had in New Jersey. It was not like that when I started there; after two years I changed everything—to improve the kitchens. At

first, we bought all our ice but I had the ice machine put in because we used so much of it for the cold-room that you could walk right into; and the room where we kept all the fish we bought, and those I caught. I remember they would come in with the ice, down the hall past the servants' dining room, right into the kitchen—everybody would stop to watch them come in (laughs). From the kitchen we had a passage into the pantry; then from the pantry a door would open into the dining room for the family. When we had our *big* dinners they would always serve the dessert in ice. I would carve the ice into some design; sometimes a fish, sometimes a doggy! (laughs) Their favorite design was of two birds—facing each other, with a bowl in between; all carved from one piece of ice I would carve it myself and make the piece just big enough for the waiter to carry. The people at those dinners would be waiting to see what I made—only the waiter didn't like it, because it was heavy to carry (laughs). It would take me two hours to carve and I was the only one in Newport to do that in those days. I learned to do the carving when I worked for Escoffier in

Chef Donon in the kitchen

London; we had a man at the Carlton Hotel who could do anything with his hands, and I would watch him. One time my handyman, Alfred, was worried about the piece I made because the dinner was very late in the evening, and he thought it wouldn't keep (laughs). After the dinner the waiter would bring it back to the kitchen and I would break it up and use the ice for the cold-room downstairs. I also had them put in a generator, for electricity, because, in 1918, my second season in Newport, we had a dinner for forty and when all was about ready to serve the lights went out. We had to get candles to finish in the kitchen, and they lighted candles in the dining room also. In those days the big houses were all lit for dinner time and sometimes the electric company in Newport could not handle the load. So I told Miss Twombly that we should have our own generator to prevent that happening again—she told me to go ahead. At the same time I had them put in a gas line from the street, so we could have new gas stoves. Many years later, I put in electric stoves but, like my kitchens in New York and New Jersey, I also kept the gas and coal—in ease we had trouble with any one of them.

There were eighteen to twenty people who would be working in the Newport house, and twelve more for the gardens. All the people who worked in the house would be coming from Florham, and two months in advance I would make arrangements to move. In the earlier days the staff would come in private railroad cars; later, I would take them in my own automobile on the Fall River boats, landing at four o'clock in the morning. A few days ahead of time two people from my department would be sent to prepare the kitchen for us. One of the maids, Nellie, an Irish girl, who worked for the family before I started, was the one who took care of Mrs. Twombly's room, and Miss Twombly's room. I would also arrange for her to go on ahead to prepare for the family.

You could not close a house that big—there was always somebody there all year to watch the place. The wife of the man who was the caretaker was also the cook for the gardeners and chauffeurs; they lived in the house between the garage and the greenhouses. Alexander Fraser was the head gardener and he lived in the lodge on Ochre Point Avenue; his cousin was the gardener for Mr. Frick in Pittsburgh—all those men were Scotch. When I started fishing in Newport, in 1917, I would go with Mr. Fraser—my fishing buddy. We had a small boat, the "Fradon", for Fraser and Donon, that we kept in the water below the house. I had a box there where I kept blackfish that I caught. The Twomblys liked that, the blackfish, but the fishermen in Newport never bothered with them. The bay was full of them years ago but they are gone now. When Fraser and I went fishing we caught so many that my wife would go all over town to give them away.

Everything we used at Vinland arrived by the Fall River boats. I had them deliver a truck-load of provisions every morning; fresh picked from the farm at Florham. The office in New York sent me a list of all the produce available from the farm at any time. We had our own train siding right on the property at Florham, and we sent everything to Hoboken where we had a special arrangement with the American Express to deliver what we needed to the houses in New York and Newport. The Express would put a truck load on the boat at night, and the next morning it would be ready at the door before we started breakfast at seven o'clock. We had our own rich milk, cream, and butter from our own dairy at Florham—we had the best ingredients!

We used to order all the chickens and poultry from Oakland Farm here in Newport—that belonged to Mrs. Twombly's nephew, William Vanderbilt. We could call the day before and the next day everything was ready for us.

Most years we were in Newport for two months, but some years the family would have all their parties in one month. All those ladies would have so many parties and dinners while in Newport, and when we did all our entertaining in one month we were *very* busy. A few times the family would *skip* Newport and go to Europe and sometimes Mrs. Twombly would be the guest of her sisters, Mrs. White, in Lenox, (Massachusetts) or Mrs. Webb, in (Shelburne) Vermont—that is when I would have my vacations. Our vacation was just before or just after the Newport season. I always had six weeks to two months' vacation every year. We traveled all over Europe and the United States, and went to France almost every other year—Mrs. Twombly would pay for those trips. She would tell me to have a good time, and after, to send the account of my expenses to the office in New York—and they would send me a check for what I spent!

And when we were in Newport we did not work at Vinland *every* day. Mrs. Twombly might go for a visit to her sisters for a week or ten days sometimes, or to visit her friend, Mrs. Ames, in Boston—and we would work at other houses in Newport to help out. All the chefs knew each other through our organization in New York and when we needed the extra help for a big dinner we could arrange with other chefs to help us if they were not working that evening. I worked many times at Marble House; and at The Breakers for Mrs. Vanderbilt, and later her daughter, Countess Szechenyi.

Things were quiet at The Breakers, at that time, and Mrs. Vanderbilt did not keep a chef on her staff year-round. She was a good friend of Mrs. Twombly. Well, her husband was Mrs. Twombly's brother. She was *always* at Vinland because it was just five minute's walk. I always arranged for a chef to work there when she needed one. One time it was a chef who worked for me at Florham when we were busy in the summer. Another time I found her a chef—oh, poor man, we used to make fun of him. He was in the war, in France, and a bullet hit him in the *behind*: We all kidded him and asked, "Where were you going when you got hit there? Were you running away?" (laughs)

Sisters Eliza Webb and Florence Twombly

Well, when he started for Mrs. Vanderbilt

40

I told him to remember that he is the chef and to assure her that he was capable of running his department by himself. You know, she wanted to keep watch on things to make sure that nothing would be wasted. When my chef went for his interview he told her that he could run his own kitchen and she said, "Who told you that?" And when he said, "It was Mr. Donon," she said, "Oh, all right!" He told me about it later—oh boy!

I worked at The Breakers a dozen times, at least—when they had two hundred or three hundred people for a party. We had a good time because of the music and the dancing. We saw that after the dinner. When I was helping out at Marble House it was owned by Frederick Prince—he was a banker and in with the Vanderbilts. I knew about the family because they lived near Prides Crossing when I came to work for Mr. Frick in 1912. So I knew the people who worked in the house.

Everything we needed at Vinland was there. I had a room in the house where I kept all our equipment when we left for New Jersey. During the 1940's they had a big war drive, and we gave all our copper pans from our houses in Newport and New York. I remember we also got all the copper from The Breakers—nearly two hundred pieces! After that, when we moved from Florham to New York or Newport, I would take just enough to use while there. I had one hundred and seventy-two pieces of copper in the kitchen at Florham—the best there was. Later, I bought some new copper pans from time to time; I always kept up with the best new equipment because they gave me enough in my budget to cover that—to modernize. After a while I had everything I needed in each house, so I didn't have to bring anything with me when we moved. You know, every year I would get a report from our office in New York that I would have "so much" surplus that I did not spend from my budget. They said if I could make any improvements to our kitchens to go ahead – but I always updated everything right along, so I would never have to use that surplus.

After Labor Day we would be on our way back to Florham where the family would stay until the middle of November, when we would move back to the house in New York, at 684 Fifth Avenue. There Mrs. Twombly gave dinners once or twice a week, for twenty-five to seventy guests— usually it was about forty people. In 1924 she bought the property at 1 East 71st Street, to build a new house there. It was because of Mr. Frick that the family built next to his house. The new house was built of light grey stone that came from Italy—it was the best material. It was a more modern design than the other houses on the Avenue. It was like a small, private, apartment house. One day Miss Twombly showed me the plans for the new house and asked me if everything was all right. I told her that the house would have no security if they built the way the architects planned it. At the old house we had ten or fifteen calls a night from the tramps who rang the bell at the service door, to beg for something to eat. When I started working at the house, at 684 Fifth Avenue, I told Miss Twombly about the tramps and she said, "My God! I didn't know about that!" I asked her if it was all right to give them something, some leftovers, if I saw they were really hungry. She said I could use my own judgement. So I always kept a piece of ham and some bread and butter; that butter came from Florham, and even without the ham it made a nice meal. We had a sandwich ready in a bag all the time and, you know, sometimes we would find the sandwich and the bag and everything on the sidewalk the next morning. Some didn't care for it I guess—imagine! Those tramps would ask at all those houses there—not just at the Twomblys. Well, I never refused anyone. One time, in 1945, after the war, a sailor came to the door during the night and he started to cry, and he asked me for $16.00, to take the train back to his home. I talked to him and felt he was telling the truth, so I gave him the money. When I got home I told my wife about it—she was surprised! Well, we never saw him again so I guess he went home as he said. At least my conscience is clear—I never forgot it, I'll tell you (laughs).

1 East 71st Street

Well, I told Miss Twombly that when we would be in the new house it would be worse because of the tramps in the Park, across the Avenue. Besides, the service entrance was used by everyone but the family; everybody came and went—some we knew and some we didn't know. A few times, at 684, we found people in the house, and one time Miss Twombly found a man in her own apartment. She was a big girl – *strong*! She asked him, "Who are you? What do *you* want? You get out of here right now!" — and she put him out! (laughs). So she asked me to talk to the architects, Warren and Wetmore, and I told them, "I'll make you a plan." I did not like the idea of telling them how to go about things because that was *their* work—but they thanked me for my suggestions and wrote me about it later. They didn't have *any idea* how things were for us in the service area. I asked them if they could put the laundry room on the roof and give us more space, so I could control the service entrance. My plan made the biggest kitchen in any house in New York; and they asked the city for a special permit to make a place under the sidewalk for our storage rooms and ice rooms. To get through the service door you had to ring a bell and you would enter and go down to a small corridor with windows on each side. On one side was the kitchen work area—on the other side was the preparation area under the sidewalk. Then you would have to ring again, to enter the kitchen. I saw to it that two people were always on duty to watch the door.

They had to redesign all that side of the building and after Miss Twombly heard from the architects she spoke to me and said, "Did you know that what you suggested will cost 'so much' to rebuild?" Well, I told her, "It is your house—you have to protect yourself."

The walls in the new kitchens were made of "Carrara Glass", from Pittsburgh. It was like marble—*very* beautiful! Both Mrs. Twombly and her daughter were very proud of it, and Miss Twombly would bring the guests down to see the kitchen. She said it was the best part of the house. So I guess she was pleased.

———————————————

Melon Rafraîchi au Kirsch
(Kirsch-flavored Honeydew)

Choose a ripe, sweet melon and, with a small knife, cut a circular plug from the stem end just large enough to permit the removal of the seeds and fibers. Clean the melon and pour into the cavity of 1/2 cup Kirsch. Replace the plug and chill the melon in the refrigerator until serving time. To serve, remove the plug and pour off the liqueur. Strain the liqueur and combine it with grenadine syrup, to taste. Cut the melon into wedges and pour a little of the Kirsch and grenadine syrup over each portion.

In 1892 Mme Nellie Melba, the Australian prima donna, gave a party at the Savoy Hotel in London. In her honor the great Escoffier created a new dessert. A swan carved of ice (to commemorate the swan in **Leohengrin***) was in the center of this masterpiece, and around it were arranged poached peaches on a bed of vanilla ice cream. Later M. Escoffier improved upon perfection by adding a puree of fresh raspberries and a sprinkling of shredded green almonds. This pêches Melba first appeared on the menu of the Carlton Hotel at its opening in London on July 15, 1989.*

A VANDERBILT HOTEL

Florham was like a private hotel for the Vanderbilts and their friends. It was the place where Mrs. Twombly had her big parties; it was perfect for that—everything was there. Beautiful gardens, the tennis court and swimming pool—all indoors: They had a stable there and some guests would go riding at six o'clock in the morning. In that building they had the big mail coaches like you will see today in the stable at The Breakers—everybody in the "400" had coaches in those days. Miss Twombly was a big woman, tall, a sportswoman. Her cousin, Harold Vanderbilt, was always there and Miss Ruth really liked him because he was a sport, like her. They had a four-horse coach and a six-horse coach at Florham, and it was Miss Twombly who would do the driving. She would drive the guests to church, and take the help to the train in those coaches. The railroad came right on the property, and the main drive to the house went under it through a tunnel—not a bad arrangement. One day Miss Twombly had an accident with the big coach, at Florham, on the road between the house and the farm. The coach was rocking from side to side and it tipped over. No one was hurt but the coach was demolished, a wreck, and she never drove again after that.

Every spring and fall Mrs. Twombly would have six big weekends at Florham. She would invite twenty-five or thirty people, mostly couples, to come for tea time on Friday and stay until after breakfast on Monday morning. Those guests would come with their own chauffeurs and maids and valets—some with their own masseur: One, a Swedish man, who fixed me up one time when I had a bad shoulder. Most people would be invited for the big dinners and we would have 125 to 150 people then; and Archer Gibson, the great organist, would come to play for the weekend guests, during dinner.

Twice a year, at Thanksgiving and at Christmas, Mrs. Twombly would have a special dinner just for the family—the Vanderbilts. It was my busiest time as I would prepare those dinners myself. Her sisters, Mrs. Webb, and Mrs. White, were always there. And other times, when Mrs. Twombly would visit at their houses for a week, or ten days, then I would have a rest. Mrs. White was Mrs.

Twombly's closest sister and after a dinner, when Miss Twombly would bring the guests down to tour the kitchen, I would always see Mrs. White there. She was always rummaging around the kitchen -you couldn't keep her out! (laughs). I remember when Mrs. Webb and her husband, Dr. Webb, came to Florham; every night I would make him a cup of beef juice. I took steak and broiled it on both sides and put it in a special device to squeeze out the juice. He would have only that at night—at

Drawing Room at Florham

8:00 o'clock. During the day he ate whatever the family had for lunch—but for dinner he took only the juice. I would always know when the Webbs would be there because Mrs. Twombly would say, "Chef, your 'patient' is coming."

The weekends were the busiest time for us, and we would begin to prepare three or four days in advance. Guests were invited weeks before— sometimes six months in advance: The family was well organized; Mrs. Twombly had her friends, and her daughter had her own. Miss Twombly was interested in clubs and would invite many guests for lunch and dinner. When I would plan for a dinner I would ask, "How many are coming, and what age?" That way I could plan something appropriate for the age group, and something special for the season. Unless they asked for a certain dish they would leave it to me to make up the menu—and we never used the same menu twice. At Florham there were luncheons and dinners for twenty to thirty guests, and every Tuesday Mrs. Twombly would invite two dozen friends, from the neighborhood, for a ladies' luncheon followed by bridge and tea. Every year we would plan a big buffet for one hundred or one hundred and fifty men who came for the cattle sales at the farm across the road. We would have to make something for every taste—to suit everyone.

Lunch was *always* at 1:30, and dinner was eight o'clock *sharp*! Mrs. Twombly would say that food is best when it is served on time. It was true—because we started a big dinner days in advance, and we had to plan *everything* if we wanted to serve it on time. We heard that if a guest was late by just five minutes they might not be invited again for months—or *years*! (laughs).

I had five people working in my department who went with me from house to house; each had a special line. One would work on the stove; another, just for the 'stocks'. I had a pastry chef, and one girl who prepared and cooked all the vegetables we received from the garden every morning. She also baked all the breads and rolls we served for breakfast. I had one man who was my handyman, my 'right-arm'; who helped to prepare the kitchens; who did the heavy work and took care of all our equipment. I hired only

Kitchen range at Florham

experienced help—people who knew what they were doing and could work, without supervision, from the orders I made for the day. I had to have people who could work on their own because I was not there to watch them all the time. I had to keep my records and manage the department. Those people who worked for me were there for twenty, twenty-four, and twenty-eight years—I made sure that they were well paid. I told the office in New York that if you pay a person well they will work harder—then you can get the 'production' from them! I gave them one full day off each week—*myself*, too! I arranged for them to have two or three days' vacation each month—and saw to it that we paid the expenses of their holidays. I would pay them myself, once a month, in cash.

You know, we had a 365-day a year job; that is how we worked. We only had time off when the family was away—visiting. Mrs. Twombly and her daughter both had a schedule and we would know weeks in advance when they would be away—so everything was well planned. I left just one person in the kitchen, to cook for the household staff, during those times. Other times I might not need everybody at Florham and would leave half my staff at the New York house, for those in the family who were staying, and take just who I needed to New Jersey; taking them in my own car, through the Lincoln Tunnel, to Florham.

Our day started at six o'clock in the morning for the guests who got up early. We had our breakfast at 7:30 a.m. and had coffee about 10:30. We took our lunch at 12:45, after preparing lunch for the household staff at noon—then we were ready to serve the family luncheon at 1:30 p.m. Every afternoon we went to our rooms to rest—to break the day in half. I had my rest from two to five o'clock every day. At six o'clock we had our dinner, then we prepared for the family dinner. Usually we worked until 8:30 or 9:00 at night, but sometimes, for a big dinner, we worked until 10:30. When the family had a dance, or musical, we stayed until 1:30 in the morning! So, you see—we earned our pay.

My staff all worked for me for many years. The longest was a Finnish girl—Sammie was her name. She still lives in New York. She started with me when she was eighteen years old and she stayed for twenty-eight years. She was the one who prepared the vegetables and baked all the things we had for breakfast. She was very friendly with my wife, and still sends me a card at Christmas and every Valentine's day!

I always knew a half-dozen people who wanted to work for me. You see, in those private houses the people advanced when they had experience—that is how I became a chef. When I needed extra help one of the chefs, from another house, would send over some people to help us out. Sammie worked at the Goelet house (Ochre Court) in Newport before I hired her. All the help at those big houses knew each other, and when she heard that I had a position open she asked for it.

When we had those big weekends at Florham I would hire five or ten extra cooks to help my regular staff; making arrangements through our chef's organization in New York. I would call, and they told me who was available. I interviewed them myself but some did not work out. They would say they could do 'so much', but after they started you could tell in a few minutes if they could do what they said. Some, I would have to let go the same day—they started in the morning and they would be gone by noon. There were people who, like today, did not care to work a full week— only a few days a week, or on the weekends, for large parties given by people like the Twomblys. The payroll was big to operate like that. The Twomblys were one of the very few families who could do that.

At the beginning of each year Miss Twombly would say, "Chef, you will have 'so much' to work with for the next twelve months to plan for it." When I began for the family I started to make a report, once a week, for our office in New York. It was a record of *current* prices on the market, for the merchandise I was buying, and the price I paid. At the office they had a record on the amount they sent me to run my department. Once a month I received a check to cover all my expenses; my pay, and also the pay for my help and everything I bought to keep the kitchens running. They told me they liked that arrangement, so I continued that way for thirty-eight years.

Croissants
(Crescent Rolls)

Dissolve the yeast in the lukewarm water and add enough of the flour to make a smooth ball of dough. Put the dough in a bowl two thirds full of warm water to rise.

Sift the remaining flour, salt, and sugar onto a pastry board. Work in the risen sponge and the milk, and mix the dough until it is smooth and firm, but not stiff. Let the dough chill for 20 minutes covered with a towel. Roll it out into a rectangle three times as long as it is wide and place in the center the butter, kneaded into a flat cake. Fold the right-hand half of the rectangle over the butter and the left half over the right, thus making three layers of dough. Turn the dough so that the open end faces you and roll it out. Repeat the folding, turning, and rolling four times more, turning the dough each time so that it is rolled out in a different direction, and chilling between the sets of two "turns" each. Chill the dough thoroughly, overnight if desired, and roll it out 1/8 inch thick. Cut strips 6 inches wide, cut the squares into triangles. Roll the triangles, beginning at the wide-end opposite the point. Shape the rolls into crescents and lay them on a lightly buttered baking sheet. Cover the pan and let the crescents rise in a warm place until they are double in bulk, about 1 hour. Brush with beaten egg yolk and bake in a hot oven (400° f.) for from 20 to 25 minutes, until they are nicely browned.

1 cake or envelope yeast
1/4 cup lukewarm water
4 cups flour
1/2 teaspoon salt
1 tablespoon sugar
1 1/2 cups milk
1 1/2 cups butter

"LIKE A QUEEN"

Once a week, at nine o'clock in the morning, Mrs. Twombly would ring for the butler, Frederick Berles, who would come for me and we would go to see her about our schedules. Every few days though, she would call me to her sitting room to talk about special things, like a birthday cake or something like that. I would sit down with her and she enjoyed that talk—she spoke to me like a <u>mother!</u> She seemed very happy. Occasionally she would ask, "Are you happy, chef? Would you

like a raise?" She had one party after another—that was her life! Oh, she *really* enjoyed life; her daughter too! Mrs. Twombly was quiet; she ate simple, not too much. She was like a *queen*! Once a week she would come to the kitchen to see me and said "good morning" to everyone. She wanted to keep in touch with all the help. She was very nice; very humble for her place. She wanted to say a few words to all my staff.

Our office in New York ran the business because the family did not wish to bother with that. Mrs. Twombly was a good businesswoman though; I guess that is why she was the favorite of her father. She did not have a secretary—her daughter did everything for her and I would see Miss Twombly every day, to discuss things like the menus I would submit one week in advance, or the staff. When I began working for the Twomblys, Miss Ruth told me that I should

Florence Vanderbilt Twombly

destroy all the records and all the menus—that she did not want any publicity on that to leak out. Both Mrs. Twombly and her daughter gave lots of money to charity without any word to the newspapers. Miss Twombly said, "You know, if we have publicity about us, life would be impossible

Lucius Beebe

here." So every week I tore everything up and burned it. I had calls all the time from those society writers in New York, Cholly Knickerbocker and the others. They were *tough*, and would call me at Florham to ask if I would tell them who were the guests in the house and what I was serving! I even had people from the newspapers in *London* call me there: Well, I would never speak to them—not *one word*! I always had someone else answer the phone, and if it was someone from the papers they were to say that I would not talk to them.

One of those society-column writers, Lucius Beebe, belonged to our Escoffier group in New York and one year, at our meeting, I gave a general invitation for everyone to come to Newport, the next summer, to go fishing with me. Well, he came and went out in my big boat, for bluefish, and after he came back to our house for lunch. In those days, before we built here, we rented a house

for the summer. Beebe went back to New York and wrote a story about me and said that I made $25,000 a year! When I heard about it I thought that I would have trouble because I did not pay taxes on that amount. I called our office to ask them if I should tell the newspapers to deny that, but they told me not to say anything about it—not *a word*. Just to forget about it, because if we denied that it would attract more attention to the family. Miss Twombly asked me about it so I told her that Beebe came fishing with me, but I never told him anything about my business and that I didn't understand why he should write that. Later, when I saw him again I asked why he wrote that, and do you know what he said? "You *live* like you make $25,000. a year! Don't take it personal, it's only a business with me." He got a bonus for that story! When I asked Miss Twombly if her mother heard about that she said, "Yes, my mother laughed. At least everyone will *think* we can afford such a chef. Our friends will have something to talk about!"

I remember, one time, there was something wrong somewhere and I asked Miss Twombly if we should speak with her mother: "Oh no, don't tell my mother—she would not want to hear about that." She was very good to her mother and I believe that Mrs. Twombly lived such a good and long life because Miss Ruth took care of most of her responsibilities.

At Florham we began the day at six o'clock in the morning. We had to start at that time because some of the guests got up early for horseback riding, so we had to be ready for them. The night before, the butler went around to ask the guests what time they would get up and what they wanted for breakfast—and if they wanted to be served in their rooms or in the dining room. You know, that is how I knew who was in the house—the butler collected the breakfast orders and gave them to me; and the names of the guests were on those cards. In those days I was only interested in my work and I was never curious about who I served, just about what they ordered for breakfast—sometimes corned beef hash! I never knew in advance who the guests would be, except when Mrs. Twombly asked for a birthday cake because I would have to put the name on it. One day though, Mrs. Twombly told me that the former king of England, the Duke of Windsor, and his wife, were coming to Florham. She asked me to prepare special things for him—he ate very plain food. She told me not to say anything to anybody because if that

Consuelo Vanderbilt

news got out the reporters would *crawl* all over the houses (laughs). It was Consuelo Vanderbilt, Mrs. Twombly's niece, who brought the Duke of Windsor, and the English nobility, to Florham.

She brought the French society also, because Consuelo was living in France at that time.

At breakfast we would serve muffins and croissants with all kinds of preserves made from the fruit we grew right on the estate. I was the one who introduced croissants here in America. I started that at the Twomblys, and everybody liked them *so much* they asked for them every day. It was the most popular thing in the Twombly house and they all copied it. Today, they serve them all over America. Miss Twombly would tell me, "Our guests eat three or four at a time!" We made lots of them because we had twenty-five or thirty people in the house every weekend. During the week, when the family was alone, Mrs. Twombly and Miss Twombly would ask just for scrambled eggs and sausages— they loved that!

The only thing that Mrs. Twombly asked for was that we give her the best of the best; she wanted a French cuisine and English style service. The head gardener and

Duke of Windsor

those people who took care of the horses and coaches were English. Mr. Tyson was the estate superintendent, and the butler was Fred Berles—and he was working for the family *before* I started in 1917. Before Frederick, the family had another butler; a tall man with a big stomach, and always a smile—the typical English butler. When he died, Miss Twombly said to me, "Oh, what will my mother do now? She liked him so much and will miss him: I am going to ask Frederick to be our butler because he knows how we want things here."

Frederick had five footmen in the pantry, all year, to serve dinner; and they wore the court livery just like they had at Buckingham Palace—only in maroon color, the Vanderbilt color. On weekends, or for those *big* dinners, Fred would have extra footmen come in from a company in New York that was in business for that purpose. At Florham they kept extra costumes, and that company always sent the same waiters because of the sizes of the costumes. I had all the food that was left over brought back to the kitchen, so we could use it later—we never wasted anything. Well, the footmen would come down to the kitchen with the extra food and we would see them come in with their maroon livery and leg stockings to their knees; it was funny to see them dressed like that. Now, I know how special that time was then, but in those days we never thought about it because that is how it was for us. In those days it was just a job for me.

Plants in the Orangerie

Those people who were guests at Florham had houses of their own, but not as well organized, and they would ask Mrs. Twombly how she ran things so smoothly. They could not get the same results—even on a smaller scale. Mrs. Twombly would say, "Go have a talk with my chef. He will tell you how to do it."—imagine! Well, Escoffier told us that if the ingredients are the best, you cannot fail. We did have the best of the best! We had all the fresh vegetables we used, right from our own gardens on the property, at Florham. And across the road, on the farm, we had big greenhouses just for vegetables out of season. I would make a list of whatever I needed for the day and give it to the gardener—and two hours later it was delivered to the kitchen door. From our greenhouses we could get melons the size of a small beach ball, and grapes the size of my thumb—one bunch would be a foot long! In the "Orangerie" we had *every* fruit—oranges, lemons, figs—everything. We used them in the kitchen. Mrs. Twombly had a big greenhouse just for flowers; she really *loved* orchids—that was her flower. She had them on the table every day. Even in Newport she had a special greenhouse for orchids. From the dairy, at the farm, we had our own rich cream and the milk that was delivered to the kitchen in one of those big cans.

All the meat we used I bought from a big supplier on Sixth Avenue in New York, Arsene Tingaud. He was the best meat supplier there. He lived on Staten Island and every morning, early, his chauffeur would drive him to the markets in New York and he would pick the best for his own business. During the Second War we raised steers and lambs on the farm, so we could be sure of our supplies. We had a butcher in Madison who took all our steers. I told him what kinds of cuts I wanted and we never ran out of anything because all the people who worked for the family gave me their ration stamps, so I had everything we needed. I *still* have some stamps I never used!

Whatever provisions we needed, that we did not grow at Florham, like meat or raw materials, spices, anything—I would order from my suppliers in New York by phone, and they would make deliveries by truck. Our office was very good to me—I would order one dozen of something, and I would get *three* dozen! I might ask for two or three bottles of special liquor, for the kitchen, and I would get a *whole case*!

At Florham they did not raise chickens, so I would order all the eggs I needed from the New York market. One day, Mrs. Twombly's grandson, William Burden, came to see me there; he was a young man at that time but he was all business; He asked me, "Chef, how many cases of eggs do you use in a year?" Well, I didn't keep track of that in my head, but I could find the records if he wanted. He said he wanted to go into business with me—he wanted to start a chicken farm on his mother's place at Mt. Kisco; and he did! He was only about seventeen years old and you could see he was going to be a businessman—a banker. I told him, "Wait, I buy all my eggs special—the chickens are fed on a certain grain." So if he wanted to do that he must feed them that way. I told him that I would only pay the market price; not higher than that—so he agreed. I bought from him for about a year and a half—then he closed his farm. I suppose he lost interest in it, so he quit. Every time he came to the house he never forgot to come down to the kitchen, before he left, to shake hands with me and to say good-bye. William Burden told me that I made him a "gourmet". It's true—he still continues with a dish I created, that I called "Terrapina la Florham"—it is haute cuisine. When I came to America I tried the terrapin dishes that they were making, but I wasn't satisfied with the results. So I experimented and found a way to make a 'stock' from the jelly from inside the shell—and I used only the black meat from the body and legs. It took three days to prepare everything, and it was not clean work. I would buy only live terrapin, and kill them in a way so they would not suffer; when they see you coming they go into their shell (laughs). One time, after I retired, Mr. Burden wanted me to make that dish for his mother's birthday, in New York. She was a lovely woman—shy, like her mother. Well, I took the live terrapin home with me, to prepare them, and my wife was afraid of them (laughs). The family liked that dish so much I was asked to make it *every week* during the winter season.

The Twomblys were very considerate of their guests, and would ask for special dishes the guests would enjoy most. Miss Twombly's best friend was Mrs. John H. Prentice, and she liked Chicken a la King—so every time she was visiting in the house I would include that in the menu. Mrs. Prentice was a lovely woman; every time she came to the house she would come to the kitchen to say hello to me, so I knew her well. She would shake my hand and pass me a five-dollar gold piece that she had in her hand (laughs). Those people who were invited to Florham could invite a guest if they wanted, and one time someone brought General Pershing for the weekend. He arrived but did not have his uniform, or even a dinner jacket. Mrs. Twombly told him, "It is all right. We *still* have the General! She made him feel right at home. Well, when he came down to dinner, and saw everybody else all dressed up—oh! He stayed that night but he left the next morning. He was embarrassed I guess (laughs).

Coeur a la Crème

The most popular dessert I made was called "Coeur a la Crème"—a dish made with cream in the form of a heart. It was my mother's recipe and the Twomblys liked it so much they asked for it *every* day, at lunch. Of course I would always have other special things for dessert, like a bowl carved from ice and filled with our own ice cream, in all kinds of shapes. Around the bowl I would make a display of strawberries on sugar branches—so you could pick them up, to eat them. But the favorite was the "Coeur", and some people would have just that for dessert.

Some funny things happened. Miss Twombly came to see me one day, and asked if there was some way to get the 'meat' from the corn—the inside, and leave the skin. So I asked a man in New York to make me a utensil, special, from my design; and he made lots of them for me. With that we made creamed corn with milk -and oh, did Miss Twombly like that! Another time, her friend, Mrs. Prentice, was there for dinner and they were serving the special corn we had late in October. She told Miss Twombly, "Don't tell me you grew this corn. I have a garden, and I have no corn myself!" Miss Twombly laughed and asked the head waiter to bring up some corn from the kitchen. When I heard about it I knew right away what must have happened. So I gave Frederick two ears of corn and he arranged them on a plate, and presented it to Mrs. Prentice (laughs). Miss Twombly had a good laugh!

Ruth Twombly's Playhouse (tennis house)

The biggest party the family ever had was when they opened the tennis house that was built for Miss Twombly—that was in October 1923. That party lasted for three days. I *never* forgot that time—we had 150 guests in the house for the dinner, and for the dance we had *six hundred*! I had to hire eight extra chefs for that weekend! On the day of the dinner and dance I began at six o'clock in the morning, and stayed until four o'clock the next morning—I almost fainted! One of my staff said to me, "Chef, what's the matter with you? Are you all right—you look white?" For those three days they had a special cover set up from the house to the tennis court building, because the party was planned six months in advance and they couldn't be sure of the weather. All those people, in their evening dress, could walk back to the house under that cover.

THE END OF AN EPOCH

Yes, Mrs. Twombly really enjoyed her life, and lived to be almost ninety-nine. One day while talking to Frederick, the butler, I said, "We must keep her alive so she can see a hundred:" Her doctor wanted her to change her diet but she told him, "You take care of my *body*—my chef will take care of my meals." I made special soufflés for her, of spinach or liver, served with fruit and vegetables, and a light dessert. I would always add a little lemon juice in everything I cooked—for the taste as well as for the digestion. You know, I cooked for the family for almost forty years, and *no one* was ever sick from the food.

Mrs. Twombly was well until the end, and the night before she died she ate a good dinner—a chicken soufflé; she was in her house at 1 East 71st Street. The next morning she died, quietly, without illness; she was alert until the end. That was on April 11, 1952, Good Friday— she was ninety-eight years old. I will never forget the day of her funeral; it was Easter Sunday, and I had a bad foot and couldn't walk, and my wife had trouble with her legs. My sister-in-law, who lived with us, was all excited and didn't know what to do until our housekeeper came back from church and helped us out. When I went to Mrs. Twombly's service I used a cane, and later that day I was back at work. The next day I was all right again.

Mrs. Twombly was wonderful to me. At Christmas she would give me something special. The office would send me a check, but it was she who gave me the gift—all the time. That last Christmas, in 1951, I remember that I

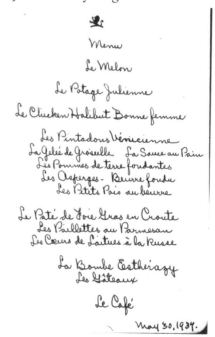

Menu written by Mrs. Donon

Table setting for Florence Vanderbilt Twombly's 1953 anniversary

was the only one of the staff she had upstairs. I got in line with all her family and friends—she lined us up! She gave me a silver service and she said, "This is for Mrs. Donon, because she does such nice work for us." She was talking about the menu cards my wife wrote out when Mrs. Twombly gave her dinners. My wife had beautiful handwriting, and she would take those cards and write out what the menu would be. The butler would place them on the dining room table between the guests. My wife would do them at home and it might take her two days to do! Sometimes it would be for twenty-five people—sometimes for a hundred and fifty!

After her mother died, Miss Twombly had a *long* talk with me. She asked me to continue to work for her, and she said that she would be away, often, so I would have lots of time off. So I told her I would stay. Miss Twombly did not entertain like her mother; it would be a dinner or a luncheon for ten or twelve people, and always the same people—her best friends.

In the summer of 1953 Miss Twombly had a special party here in Newport, at Vinland, to celebrate her mother's coming anniversary—the Duke of Windsor was there! Just before a dinner I would come up and go to the dining room to see how everything looked. When we had *that* party I arranged for my sister-in-law to be there with her camera. I asked her to follow me into the dining room, but not to say anything to anybody—not a word -just come in with me and take a picture. When Mrs. Twombly celebrated a birthday I would always make the cake myself. It was a kind of sponge cake with white icing, very

Ruth Twombly's Playhouse pool

light, we call it "biscuit" in French. They had a big silver tray with feet on it, like a stand, to hold the cake. I always made the cakes as big as the tray because there were about thirty people for those parties—the whole family. The person whose birthday it was would have their name on the cake, such as, "To Mrs. Twombly", and they would always cut the first piece and then the butler would take it and cut pieces for everyone else. Mrs. Twombly always asked for just one candle on a birthday cake; she said, "Every year is just one more year—so, one candle only." I still have some candles she used.

During the winters, when Mrs. Twombly was still living in New York, Miss Ruth would spend a couple of days a week at Florham, at the tennis court. She had two bedrooms and a sitting room there and she liked it because she was close to her tennis and the pool. Miss Twombly entertained her friends there—always four ladies. There was a small kitchen in that building and I would make up a <u>big</u> basket of food for them, and arrange for one of my staff to be there. The main house was always kept open for guests and for the help, because we kept all our staff. It would be impossible to close Florham, even for short periods, because of all the people who worked there. The three houses were kept up, and in full operation, until Miss Twombly died.

The last time I saw her was when she was leaving the house in New York, for France, in 1954. Every time she left the house for a trip I would come up from the service entrance and say good-bye to her—she *liked* that. She would say, "Good-bye chef, I'm going to see your country." The last time she left, in 1954, I didn't *know* it would be the last time; I went out to see her as she got into her car. I knew she was under the doctor's care, and she was not well, but she felt good because she was going to Paris; she said she would be gone for about a month. Three weeks later, on September 1st, she died—in the dining room of the Ritz Hotel. Both Miss Twombly and her mother loved Paris and always stayed at the Ritz—it was the best in Paris, and right on the Place Vendome. She was only seventy-two years old. She was tall, like her father, and had a good appetite—she could eat a whole duck by herself! I guess she died of good living—she had a good life.

I left in March, 1955. It took us six months to close the houses and during that time Mrs. Twombly's other daughter, Mrs. Burden, and her son, William Burden, gave some special dinners at the houses in New York and New Jersey. They stayed a few weekends there, at Florham, before we closed up—so I kept all my staff until March.

In those last few months I made an inventory of all the equipment we had in New York, at Vinland, and at Florham; everything went to Mrs. Burden's house in Mt. Kisco, New York. I know because, later, William Burden's chef came to see me about a special dish I made, and he told me that the place looked "like a store!"—everything the Twomblys had was there. I had packed it all, *myself*, and we sent it to Mt. Kisco. It must be like a small Florham there because they have greenhouses and a farm.

After Miss Twombly died I found that the family left me enough to retire on. When the reporters heard about that they tried to find out how much—they called me on the phone many times to ask, but I never talked to them. William Burden told me, "Forget about it!" That was the understanding—it was part of the job.

CRABES A LA DIABLE
(DEVILED CRABS)

Meat of 1 dozen hard-shell crabs (about 1 1/2 pounds meat)
1 tablespoon butter
1/2 tablespoon flour
2 cups hot milk
1 onion, chopped
1/2 cup fresh bread crumbs 2 tablespoons cream
1 teaspoon chopped parsley

Melt the butter, stir in the flour and cook the roux for a minute, stirring constantly with a wooden spoon. Add the hot milk and the onion, chopped, and cook for 10 minutes, stirring from time to time. The sauce should be thin. Add the cream, a little salt and pepper to taste, breadcrumbs, crabmeat and parsley. The mixture should be thick enough to hold its shape. If necessary, add more breadcrumbs. Fill prepared crab shells or individual scallop dishes with the crab mixture, mounding it high. Mix some dry mustard to a paste with water and brush the filled shells with it. Sprinkle with breadcrumbs and with melted butter and brown quickly in a hot oven. Serve bubbling hot.

"CHEZ-NOUS"

The day after I retired I felt good! I didn't have to get up early for work, and I didn't have to think about any business other than my own.

When I was working for the Twomblys I never thought I would be living here in Newport one day. We talked about building for years, my wife and I. We had relatives in France and we talked about when I would retire and where we would live. We had a monument, near Paris, for our family, because we thought we would be living there some day. Well, later we decided to stay here, and I'm glad now.

Our New York apartment was at 175 East 79th Street, on the third floor. We moved there in 1931 because my mother-in-law, Mrs. Blaudin, and my wife's sister, Estelle (Blaudin), were with us and we wanted a bigger place. It was a beautiful building and we had two bedrooms, a big living room and a dining room, a kitchen, a bath, and a maid's room; we kept that apartment until 1960.

During the time I was working in Newport we rented a house here, for two months, every summer, because we had friends from New York coming to stay with us—my wife's family, too. I had a boat built specially for me—thirty-two feet long. It had a toilet and two beds inside—outside there was room for ten people. I called it the "Mon Plaisir" ("My Pleasure"). I kept it for fifteen years, until 1947. It was expensive at that time but, well, that was all right because I was working—that was my pastime, fishing. I told my wife, "What else can I do? I don't drink or gamble. I have to have something to fit in with my time." Because I worked almost every day, and evening. I went fishing every morning between four and seven o'clock, and sometimes, when I had the afternoon off, we went as far as the Cape Cod Canal. One time I had a twenty-pound bass on my line and I had him near the boat. I saw a shark fin come, and *bang*—he took half my fish I pulled in the bass and I got just the head—the shark got the best part (laughs).

Here in Newport the "400" would go to the Gooseberry Island Club because it had the best bass fishing on the coast. I went there with my boat because I knew the caretaker. In the big hurricane of 1938 it all went! They gave the island to Newport Hospital, to sell, and I bid on it—I wanted it for the fishing there, but a very rich man got it. Later, I sold my boat to him because I started fishing from the rocks and I liked it better.

So, in 1947, we decided we would build here and I bought two lots on Easton's Point—facing Vinland and The Breakers. It was the first modern house built in that area—in 1947 it was still farmland. The builder was a friend of mine, we would go fishing together, and I asked him to build the house. I told him, "Make a good job of it and put in everything you can think of now, because I have the extra money." Later, in 1957, we had the veranda built over the garage. We love to watch the sunset from there—the sky is like fire; it's *beautiful*! At night you could hear the music when they had parties in those big houses across there, on the Cliff Walk. I told my builder to hire the same man, Spingler, who worked for the Twomblys, to paint our house. I met him there, at Vinland, many times, so I wanted him to do the painting. In the summer of 1948 we asked them to finish only one room, so we could move in, and it wasn't all finished until after April in 1949.

Miss Twombly heard about our house from the caretaker at the Clambake Club, who lived right across the road here. The next morning, when we were talking about the business of the day, she told me that she heard about it and asked why I built there. I said that I had been all over the world and

Mon Plaisir with (left to right) Mr. Donon; Mr. Boucher, supertindent of Ochre Court estate; Alexander Fraser, superintendent of Vinland; Arsenè Tingaud, purveyor of fine meats in New York City

decided to stay here because I can fish when I retire. She asked me to invite her to visit when the house was finished. Well, she came one day with her chauffeur and footman—in her Rolls Royce! Do you know what she said? "You are lucky. I would rather live in *your* house than mine." I asked her why she would say that, and she answered, "Because I don't have any privacy over there.", looking in the direction of Vinland. "I envy you. You can go where you want to and do what you want, and nobody is watching you all the time." You know, it was true. When Miss Twombly wanted something she had to ring for the footman—everybody was watching her to see if she wanted anything. And she said that she envied me!

Chez Nous (west and south view)

People thought that the Twomblys paid for our house. After they died some people came here and asked, "When will the house be for sale? They are closing the Twombly estate." They thought it was part of the estate – imagine!

My wife and Estelle were good housekeepers. When we built they bought everything we needed here in the house. Now, when we need something, we look and find what we need—the drawers are full! We never needed to buy anything else.

Mrs. Donon and her sister got along well together. There were no children, so her sister kept her company. Estelle was her mother's favorite. When their mother died I was with her and she asked me to promise I would keep the sisters together. Estelle was always very close to my wife, and even when I worked for Mr. Frick she was always there when I went to visit Charlotte—to watch me! (laughs). She was a hairdresser and ran the beauty parlor at the Copley Plaza Hotel in Boston; and later, in New York, she continued in private practice only. She kept all her equipment in the apartment, and when she would go to the society people on Fifth Avenue, to fix their hair, they would send their chauffeurs for her—even from their places in the country! After Estelle retired, in 1945, she kept a few of her customers, like Mrs. Prince, who would call up and ask her to come to Marble House to do her hair. They liked her very much and tipped her good for that! So she knew everybody.

She started to take pictures before I met the family, and she followed that all her life. When I think of it now, I wish my sister-in-law had taken some pictures of the special dishes we made for those big dinners. They were works of arts. Pictures of the footman too, when they came down with the dishes. She could have stayed in the kitchen, and I could have called her when I was ready, and nobody would have said anything. The only thing I did was to have her take those pictures of that anniversary cake, here in Newport. Now, I think how *special* the time was then. But in those days it was just a job to me.

My wife, and her sister, bought everything there was, and everything new, for cameras. They loved to take pictures, and when they needed film or supplies they never bought only one of each but a dozen of each—more sometimes. They only bought the best and I paid for all that—the

Chez Nous living room

bill came to me! (laughs). Estelle took pictures for everybody. It was not a job for her, she did it because she loved it. After she retired she took pictures almost every day! In 1949 we had the builder make a darkroom here, downstairs, because she always developed and printed all her pictures herself—and my wife and I took films, as a hobby, starting with the Colonial Exposition, near Paris, in 1931. After a trip it would take me almost two months to put them all together. To edit them and put in the titles, on my free time.

We put flowers all around the house here. We have roses all over the fence, and I planted blue pines and Russian olive bushes that smell so sweet when they bloom. The hydrangeas we have in front, we have two of them, they were given to us by a boy from France that we sent to school here in America. And I have my little garden where I grow some vegetables and herbs. Yes, we all had the time of our lives here. We were lucky to be old and still enjoy ourselves.

The Donon's 50th Anniversary in 1964

Mr. Joseph Donon

629 WOLCOTT AVENUE
MIDDLETOWN, RHODE ISLAND
U. S. A.

THE BEST OF THE BEST

CHEF DONON PROFILED IN *THE NEW YORKER*

This profile, written by Geoffrey T. Hellman, appeared in the March 10, 1962 issue of The New Yorker

Joseph Donon

Joseph Donon, the most famous and very likely, the richest private chef or ex-chef, in the world, retired from employment by the Twombly Estates, 20 Exchange Place, in the spring of 1955, when he was sixty-seven. He had been on the payroll of the same family for thirty-eight years—ever since April 2, 1917, when he became *chef de cuisine* or head cook, to Mrs. Hamilton McK. Twombly, daughter of William H. Vanderbilt, on whose farm at New Dorp, Staten Island, she was born, and granddaughter of the second, and first rich, Cornelius Vanderbilt, the most famous ex-ferryboat proprietor in the world. At the time Donon entered her service, she had three houses; a red brick one, with about sixty rooms, at 684 Fifth Avenue, on Fifty-fourth Street; one near Convent Station, New Jersey, which had a hundred rooms and was inspired, architecturally, by the part of Hampton Court Palace that was designed by Sir Christopher Wren; and a Newport villa, in the Tudor style, with fifty rooms. In 1926, having sold her town house to John D. Rockefeller, Jr., who owned the house next door, she built a white stone, Carrère and Hastings seventy-roomer seventeen blocks up the Avenue, at 1 East Seventy-first

Street. Characterized by the late Dixon Wecter in this book "The Saga of American Society" as "vastly rich, proud, frosty," but (as we shall see) a democratic and warm-hearted heroine to her chef, she was the leading hostess and dominant Old Guard figure of that society during the years that Donon had charge of her kitchens and of the multifarious and elaborate menus, invariably written out in French, that issued therefrom. She died in New York on April 11, 1952, at an age that the *Times* placed at ninety-four in its obituary but has upped to ninety-eight in subsequent references. Miss Ruth Vanderbilt Twombly, one of her two surviving daughters (a son and another daughter died in their teens), had lived with her all her life, keeping house for her most of that time, and she retained the chef until *her* death, at seventy-two, in the fall of 1954, after which he remained in the service of the family, or its estates, for a final six months, closing up the New York house and the Jersey house, and cooking a few dinners for William A. M. Burden, a grandson of Mrs. Twombly, in one or another of the three places *he* owned. (The Newport villa was later given to Salve Regina College by Mr. Burden's mother, Mrs. William A. M. Burden, Sr., the former Florence Vanderbilt Twombly, who had inherited it from *her* mother.) Mr. Burden urged Donon, who is an Officer of the French Legion of Honor and the author of a cookbook, "The Classic French Cuisine," to carry on as a permanent fixture of his threefold ménage, but Donon had worked over hot stoves since he was thirteen, he was comfortably off, and he owned a house in Middletown, Rhode Island, just outside Newport, called villa Chez-Nous, where he wanted to spend more time *chez lui* so he quit.

Last fall, I got in touch with this deserving senior citizen—a short, stocky man, pink-cheeked, black-browed, and white-mustached, who is, at seventy-three, firm of chin and full of bounce—to find out how he was taking his ease. His current major interests were speedily revealed as Les Amis d'Escoffier Society of New York, a dues-paying band of *Feinschmecker* (two *serviette-au-cou* dinners a year), with affiliated chapters in seventeen other American cities, which described itself as "a non-commercial, non-profit seeking fraternity of true Epicures constituted to perpetuate the memory of the great Chef, Auguste Escoffier, and to promulgate the doctrine of a greater appreciation of the art of good living," and of which Donon is a co-founder and the executive vice-president; its offshoot, Les Amis d'Escoffier Society Foundation, Inc., a tax-exempt organization that awards scholarships to help cooking-school students keep on studying, of which he is a co-founder and the president; the Auguste Escoffier Foundation Museum and Gastronomic School of Villeneuve-Loubet, Alpes-Maritimes, Provence, of which he is a co-founder and the executive chairman; Les Médaillés Militaires de New York, a branch of a Paris-centered association of war veterans who have been decorated with the Médaillé Militaire, the highest French military medal, awarded for distinguished service in action, which raises funds to help support orphans of Médaillés, and of which he is president, having acquired the status of a Médaillé during the First World War; and salt-water fishing, in which he engages before breakfast most mornings during the June-to-October season at Sachuest Point, an eight-minute drive from Villa Chez-Nous. However, since these interests are rooted in Mr. Donon's earlier days, and since, in any case, sharing his recollection pleases him, my curiosity led to a review not only of his present mode of life but of his Twombly, and even pre-Twombly, past.

The recollections were imparted at a series of lunches, none of them cooked by Mr. Donon. His co-founder of the various Escoffier groups is Mr. Claudius C. Philippe, execute vice-president of Loew's Hotels, of which the latest is the Summit, and this connection, together with the circumstance that Mr. Donon had invited his associate to join us, led to the selection of the new hotel's Gaucho Room as our first meeting place. "I was very fond of fishing in the neighborhood of Chantilly, in the valley of the Oise, where I passed my childhood, and where fishing and hunting are among nature's blessings," Mr. Donon said as, without waiting for Mr. Philippe to arrive, he ordered consommé, minute steak, blueberry pie, and a bottle of Burgundy, "but my real fishing—salt water—began in Newport in 1917, during the first summer I was with Mrs. Twombly. I fished then before going to work, so I got up at about three in the morning, and I still do, since it's the best time of day for fishing. Mrs. Twombly was at Newport—her villa there was called Vinland—from July 1st to Labor Day. From Labor Day until Thanksgiving we were in New Jersey, from then until May in New York, and in May and June back in Jersey. But all three houses were kept open all the time, for occasional visits. The Jersey place was called Florham—a combination of the first syllable of Mrs. Twombly's first name, Florence, and the first syllable of the first name of her husband, a Bostonian, who dies several years before I joined her staff—and it included a sixty-foot orangery; a five-hundred-acre farm, and hothouses for flowers, other fruits, and vegetables; all in all, it covered nine hundred and twenty-one acres, which are now taken up partly by Fairleigh Dickinson University, partly by a Standard Oil engineering center, and partly by a local high school. There were thirty-two on the staff inside the house—five in the kitchen for the family alone, plus five footmen in the pantry—and eighty outside. Mrs. Twombly and her daughter had anywhere from a dozen to thirty guests—couples, mostly—every weekend; in the early days, many of them came from New York on a special train hired by their hostess. Weekends were Friday to Monday, and house guests were invited at least six weeks, and often several months, in advance. A month ahead of time, I'd be told how many of them to expect, and also how many guests there would be just for lunches and dinners, so that I could plan the menus accordingly. On large weekends, we fed as many as a hundred and fifty; on one, sometime in 1920, I think, when the new tennis-court building was opened—it had an indoor court, a swimming pool, dressing rooms for men and ladies, a kitchen, and living quarters for two servants, and it was connected with the main house, two hundred yards away, by a covered walk—we had a hundred and fifty for meals all weekend and a Sunday-night buffet supper at the court for six hundred. Miss Twombly was fond of tennis. She was a good player—a tall girl, well built, the English type—and on visits to Florham after her mother's death she stayed in the tennis-court building. I set up a budget at Florham, of course, but no limit was placed on my expenses, Mrs. Twombly knew cooking, and she knew wines; entertaining was her life, and she lived for it. Her maître d'hotel, Fred Berles, took care of the cellar, which was chosen by Miss Twombly. Berles was there when I came, and stayed until after Miss Twombly's death. I had people with me eighteen, twenty-four, twenty-eight years. Mrs. Twombly was a perfect lady. The first thing after breakfast, she'd come into the kitchen, say hello to everybody, and then tell me, 'Your dinner last night was very nice,' or something of the sort. Then she'd say something complimentary to the other members of the staff. That's all she *would* say."

After pausing for a bite of steak, Mr. Donon went on, "In 1945, we had another large weekend, at Newport, when a ball was given for the Duke and Duchess of Windsor and we served a dinner for eighty-five, featuring, Lobster Lafayette. This is a dish that I introduced formally in 1941 at a five-course subscription dinner held at the Waldorf by the Coordinating Council of French Relief Societies. Miss Anne Morgan, a founder of American Relief for France, who was a frequent guest at Mrs. Twombly's, asked me to take charge of the meal, and I rounded up four other French chefs— Joseph M. Frédérique, of the World Wool Club; Domonique Dorratcague, of the Knickerbocker Club; Lucien Toucas, of the Astor; and Gabriel Lugot, of the Waldorf—and each of us prepared one of the five courses. Dorratcague, Toucas, and Lugot were all *anciens combatants*, too. Frank Crownshield, another frequent Twombly guest, made the social arrangements, and during the coffee he presented the five of us to the four hundred people at the dinner."

I asked Mr. Donon what about the distinguished mark of Lobster Lafayette.

"The ingredients," he said. "The way the melted butter, chopped onions, tomatoes, olive oil chopped shallots and garlic cloves, cognac, white wine, parsley, and bay leaves are combined in the cooking of the lobster, and the sauce—fish *velouté*, flavored with tarragon and cognac— that is poured over them as they rest in a bed of pilaf. Garnish with a slice of truffle warmed in butter and serve very hot."

I said I'd do my best.

"During the week, when we were at Florham," Mr. Donon continued, "Mrs. Twombly gave luncheons and dinners for from eighteen to thirty-two; on Tuesdays she had a luncheon for twenty-four ladies residing in the surrounding countryside, followed by bridge and tea. She was always on time for meals, and she liked others to be punctual. She would not wait for anyone. This is always much appreciated by a chef, since time is of the essence serving a dinner. Before lunch and dinner, very tiny hors d'oeuvres, hot and cold, were served, with beverages, in the salon. Although this is thought to be done to build up an appetite, Mrs. Twombly's purpose was to assemble all the guests, so that they would be ready to enter the dining room at the exact time set for the meal. Dinner

Homard Lafayette

Melt the butter and in it cook the chopped onions until they are soft but not brown. Add the tomatoes, peeled, seeded, and chopped, and cook all together slowly, in a covered pan, for 2 hours.

Sever the tails and claws from the bodies of the lobsters. Boil the bodies in salted water for 10 minutes and clean them well under running water. Set them aside.

Heat the oil in a sauté pan and cook the lobsters tails and claws over high heat, stirring constantly, until they turn red. Pour off the cooking oil. Sprinkle the lobster with the shallots and garlic, both chopped, and cook, covered for 5 to 10 minutes. Add half the cognac, blaze it, and put out the fire by covering the pan. Add the white wine, simmer for a few minutes, and add the previously prepared tomato and onion mixture, the parsley, and the bay leaf. Cover the pan again and cook slowly for 20 to 25 minutes. Turn the contents of the pan into a colander and strain the liquid into a bowl. When the tails and claws are cool enough to handle, remove the meat whole by cutting the shells with a scissors. Put the lobster meat in a sauté pan and sprinkle it with 2 tablespoons of the cooking liquid. Cover the pan and set it in a warm place.

Force the remaining contents of the colander through the sieve and combine this with the cooking liquid. Reduce the mixture over high heat to about 1 ½ cups.

Make 1 cup chicken velouté, add the tarragon and the remaining cognac, and pour a little sauce over each body. Garnish with a slice of truffle warmed in butter. Serve very hot.

3 tablespoons butter
3 onions
12 ripe tomatoes
6 1-pound lobsters
½ cup olive oil
6 shallots
3 garlic cloves
2 cups dry white wine
½ cup cognac 3 sprigs parsley
1 bay leaf
1 teaspoon chopped tarragon
1 cup velouté sauce 2 cups rice
6 slices truffle

was at eight-thirty, and there were often midnight suppers that went on until the small hours of the morning. Mrs. Twombly's houses were very well organized; she was a wonderful business woman. I understand that in this she resembled her grandfather, Commodore Vanderbilt. Her cellar was so greatly expanded just before prohibition that many wines purchased at that time were still there when she died. During the Second World War, when meat was rationed, and for some time thereafter, steers were raised on the farm at Florham for home consumption. Mrs. Twombly cautioned me never to buy on the black market, and I never did, and, indeed, I had little occasion to, for we had our own milk and cream from the farm, our own vegetables, raised both outdoors and in, and our own fruit—grapes, melons, nectarines, and so on—from the greenhouses. We baked all our own bread, rolls, pastry and cake; *croissants* were served with every meal. We never bought much of anything outside, in fact, except raw materials. Mrs. Twombly had drawn upon Sherry for supplementary catering for big parties before I came, but I dispensed with this. It's more satisfactory if you do everything yourself."

I asked what Mrs. Twombly liked to eat besides Lobster Lafayette, tiny hors d'oeuvres, steers, and *croissants*, and my companion, looking something like a minatory lobster himself, waggled a finger at me.

"She and her daughter were not particular about their own meals," he said. "Those two were in perfect health—until Mrs. Twombly's extreme old age. They had no regime; they ate anything. They simply liked the best of the best. The menus were planned to please their guests. Mrs. Twombly's desire to please her friends was touching. If a certain guest had a liking for a certain dish, I would be asked to include it. When Mrs. John H. Prentice, her best friend, was expected, I knew that it meant Chicken à la King. If a guest had a birthday during his or her stay, I would be asked to make a birthday cake. Breakfasts, served from seven to ten either on trays in the bedroom suites or in the breakfast room, to which mostly the men came down, were à la carte: choice of fruit; cooked or dry cereals; eggs in any form; with *croissants*, brioches, hot muffins, biscuits, or toast; chicken hash; brown hash; creamed hash; fish balls; sausages; and all the rest. Lunch, after the hors d'oeuvres, usually started with borsch, madrilène, clear okra, vichyssoise, Crème Indienne, or Crème Santé, or Homard à la Parisienne, with mayonnaise sauce, all served cold. Next, there might be Chair de Crabes à la Diable, Crabmeat and Oyster Crabs Newburg, Soft-Shell Crabs Meunière, or among egg dishes, Oeufs Bénédictine, Oeufs Opéra, Soufflé d'CEufs Aurore, Oeufs Mollets, or Oeufs Gratinés à la Niçoise, followed by Supremes de Volaille à l'Ancienne, Supremes de Volaille à la Virgineenne, Poulet Grillé Diable à l'Americaine, Escapoles de Veau à la Viennoise, Chicken à la King, Tournedos Rossini, Volau-Vent à la Toulousaine, or Ris de Veau Financïere. Desserts, at lunch and dinner, included hot and cold souffles, Bombe Glacée Pralinée, Café Parfait, and Petites Glaces Parisiennes. The most popular dessert was Coeur à la Crème—freshly made cream cheese in the shape of a heart, accompanied by fresh strawberries. The richness of the farm's milk and cream made possible an extreme delicacy in this *couer*. Such a source of supplies is an enormous asset to a chef."

"What was for dinner besides these desserts?" I asked Mr. Donon as he started on the Gaucho blueberry pie.

"It was customary to begin with fresh beluga caviar served on ice with blinis," he said. "Then there might be melon, or oxtail soup. Terrapin was served in season, and other specialties were Homard Lafayette, Homard à la Madras, Homard Newburg, and Truites à la Nage, Sauce Verde. For the main course, Baron d'Agneau aux Primeurs, Filet de Boeuf Richelieu, Selle de Veau Orloff, or Poularde Soufflée Princesse, followed, during the game season, by pheasant, partridge, woodcock, quail, or wild duck or, out of season by Pâté de Foie Grass au Vin de Porto, Poularde Rose de Mai, Caneton à la Viosin, or Jambon de Virginie. Then again, a cheese soufflé might be served after the main course. Mrs. Twombly was especially fond of soufflés."

Resolving to brush up on my French, I offered my host a cigar, which he declined. I asked him what he caught à la pêche.

"Stripers," he said. "Striped bass. On the morning of June 18, 1958, casting in the surf with menhaden, I took one that weighed sixty-three and three-quarter pounds. It was fifty-four inches long and thirty-two inches in girth. I think it's the fifth-heaviest striped bass ever taken with sporting tackle in this country. I spent nearly an hour landing that one. I don't like to fish from a boat; the real sport is casting. I fish with one or the other of two neighbors—a retired Navy man, and a Navy commander on active duty at Quonset. At four every morning in the season, you can find me on the rocks at Sachuest Point, baiting the water with chum. This brings the fish in around five. Do you know how many stripers I caught last season? A hundred and fifty—one of them a thirty-six-pounder. The Rhode Island Development Council, in Providence, has put out a poster to attract tourists to Rhode Island, and on it is a picture, taken four or five years ago, that shows me holding up a forty-nine-pound stripper I had just landed."

My Donon said he was back from fishing by seven, and I asked what he did then.

"Have breakfast and go to bed," he said "*Café au lait* with a brioche or a *croissant*. After an hour, I get up, absolutely fresh, and I spend the morning attending to my correspondence or chatting with my wife. We have no children. We're both interested in the Alliance Française de Newport, which every April sponsors a contest—an essay and an oral examination—among pupils who are studying French in the local high schools, with a first prize of an eight-week trip to France, two hundred-dollar prizes, and one fifty-dollar prize. I also work in my garden. We had our house built fourteen years ago on two big lots that used to be a farm; it has thousands of roses and a great many trees around it, and we're surrounded by water on three sides. We used to rent a house in Newport. Here in New York, we had an apartment on East Seventy-ninth Street for thirty years; we gave it up only last spring. In New Jersey, I shared a house near Florham with another couple. My wife is from Boston, of French parentage; we were married in 1914, when I was *chef de cuisine* to Henry Clay Frick in his houses in New York, Pittsburgh, and Prides Crossing, on the Massachusetts North Shore. It's funny, I kept working for people who had three houses. I'll come back to Mr. Frick in a minute. My big meal at the Villa Chez-Nous is lunch; hors d'oeuvres, an entrée, and a dessert—Croute Parisienne aux Fruits is my favorite. Then, after a nap, I call on friends, receive friends, or take a walk. I like to look at trees and flowers. I wanted to be a florist when I was a boy, but I was a sickly child, and terribly fussy about food, and my father advised me to become a chef, so I could cook my own meals. 'Flowers will only give you hay fever," he said. I take a light supper—vegetable soup, salad, cheese, and fruit—and I'm in bed by eight, unless we're having a dinner party. Our dining room seats ten. I have a glass or two of wine with lunch and dinner; rosés are my favorite, and my favorite rosé is a good Tavel. I don't do much cooking myself—my wife likes to cook, and we also have a maid who is a wonderful cook—but I set the menus, and if we are having friends in for a meal and I want something a little complicated, such as a Coq au Vin, Escargots à la Bourguignonne, or a Quiche Lorraine, I do it. Once a week, I make a blueberry pie. I think it's the nicest thing we have in America."

"How about Mr. Frick?" I asked as Mr. Donon poured a second cup of coffee.

"Well, that takes me back to Escoffier, and, really, to the very beginning," he said. "My father had a dairy farm at Chantilly and was also in the transportation business there. He was a friend of Antoine Ott, who had once been the chef of the Duc d'Aumale, owner of the Chateau de Chantilly, and when I was thirteen, Mr. Ott, who then owned the Hotel des Arenes in Senlis, gave me an apprenticeship in the hotel kitchens. When I showed an aptitude for cooking he sent me to the Maison Gervaise, a large bakery in Vincennes, where I learned my pastry. My father paid a hundred francs for one year's tuition. For the next six months, the bakery paid me a hundred francs a month. After that, I worked for eight months as an assistant chef at the Mexican Embassy, in Neuilly, and then became assistant to the chef of the Marquis de Panisse-Passis, at Villeneuve-Loubet, which, of course, was Escoffier's birthplace. Escoffier himself was then at the Carlton Hotel in London, but one day while he was on vacation he came to lunch with the Marquis, at a time when the chef was away, also on vacation. So I cooked the meal, and after it was over, the Marquis called me in and introduced me to his guest. 'If you're ever in London, come and see me,' Escoffier said. I was seventeen. Six weeks later, when we were back in Paris—the Marquis had a house there, and, yes, a third one, in the Vallée de Chevreuse—I resigned and went to London, where, taking Escoffier at his word, which I don't think he had expected, I went to see him at the Carlton. He laughed — at my youthful impulsiveness, I suppose—and said I could work for him during the season. That was in 1905, and I stayed there five years, working summers in hotels in Evian-les-Bains. In those days, the Carlton had seventy chefs and served two hundred dinners every night, with everything cooked to order. In 1910, I had to leave to put in two years of military service back home, but when that was over I returned to the Carlton. Almost at once—it was in March, 1912—Escoffier asked me to look after a special dinner for twenty that Mr. Frick was going to give in a private room. Escoffier made the menu and I cooked it—Mousse de Sole à l'Américaine as the entrée and Poularde Soufflée Princesse for the main course. Frick called me in afterward, gave me two twenty-dollar gold pieces as a tip—I'd never seen a gold piece before, and at first I thought they were medals—and said, 'Would you like to come to America as my chef?' I said yes. We were booked to sail on the Titanic two days later, but then Mrs. Frick sprained her ankle, so we changed to the North German Lloyd liner Amerika, sailing two days after that. We passed the wreckage of the Titanic on the way, and the iceberg as well, our captain having changed his course in order to do so. Mr. Frick paid my passage, but the immigration restrictions did not permit an American who hired a foreign servant abroad to bring him into the country simply as part of his retinue, so technically I came here on my own, stating that I planned to become a resident. To be admitted on that basis, you had to have two hundred and fifty dollars, and since I had no savings, I borrowed the money from a friend in London. When we docked, at Hoboken, I didn't see Mr. or Mrs. Frick on the pier, because I'd been traveling second class while they, of course, were in first, and by the time I got through with the immigration routine, they had gone. I hadn't thought to ask Mr. Frick for his address, and he probably assumed I'd learned it from somebody else. My English was poor, but finally I found a taxi and said, 'I am going to Henry Clay Frick in New York.' 'Who is that?' the driver asked. 'A rich man,' I told him, so the driver said, 'He must be living on Fifth Avenue. We'll stop at every block and ask.' The Frick house then was at 640 Fifth Avenue—it was later Mrs. Cornelius Vanderbilt's—and, by luck, when we made our first stop we were only a block away, at Fiftieth Street. The driver asked a man on the sidewalk where Mr. Frick lived, and the man pointed and said, 'Right there.' I left for Prides Crossing that night, and the next morning I was told there were to be twenty for lunch. Fortunately, although Escoffier had been mad at me for leaving him, he had given me some good advice. 'Americans don't know how to run a house. You'll have to tell *them*.' So I wasn't rattled. Frick paid me a hundred and fifty dollars a month and a hundred a month personal expenses, so I was able to save my entire salary."

I asked Mr. Donon what Mr. Frick liked to eat.

"Broiled lobster, scallops, and three-inch steaks," he said. "He had sixty in help. He appeared to be a little rough on the surface, but that was deceptive. He was like a father to me. He told me how to invest my savings, and five or six years after I came here, when my father died and left me and my two brothers forty thousand dollars a piece, I again got his financial recommendations—

this time through his chauffeur, because by then I was working for Mrs. Twombly. I still have U.S. Steel that I bought between 1912, and 1919. There have been several splits, and my stock now is worth quite a few times what I paid for it. Mr. Frick's son, Childs Frick, then in his twenties, was an explorer—he is now an honorary trustee of the Museum of Natural History—and he once came back from Africa with a pygmy, who became a house guest at Prides Crossing for a while. I made some special dishes for him."

"What sort?" I asked.

"All kinds of rice, grain, vegetable roots, and broiled steak," Mr. Donon said. "Mr. Frick's daughter, Miss Helen Frick, who was eighteen when I came here, used to help me with my English. She spoke perfect French. *'Quels sont vos ennuis, chef?'* she would say. Oh, when I heard that French I was happy."

As Mr. Donon pushed his empty pie plate away, we were joined by Mr. Phillipe. He was lucky that Mrs. Twombly was not giving the lunch, for he was an hour late. As matters stood, though, he had no difficulty in ordering a minute steak. Then, leaning back in his chair, he said, "It's hard to find a good private chef today. Jack Heinz is looking for one, to travel with him, and is willing to pay twenty thousand dollars a year, but he hasn't found one yet."

"French chefs—many of them, like myself, pupils of Escoffier—were numerous in America in the early nineteen hundreds," Mr. Donon said. "But during the First World War most of them returned to France to fight, and most of those never came back here. Phillipe—his father, as you may know, was a great chef, at the Carlton Club in London—helped me to organize Les Amis d'Escoffier Society, at the Waldorf, in 1936. We now have two hundred members in Greater New York and more than a thousand in other cities. There's a ladies' chapter in Boston. In New York, we give a Diner d'Automne and a Diner de Printemps. We started the Society's Foundation seven years ago, at the Beverly Hilton, in Los Angeles. Founder members, pay five thousand dollars outright, in lieu of all subsequent dues. Patron members pay two hundred and fifty dollars a year, contributing members one hundred, sustaining members twenty-five, and ordinary members ten. So far, we have disbursed over twelve thousand dollars for cooking scholarships. In 1959, we organized the Escoffier Foundation in France. One of the Escoffier's grandsons, Dr. J.B. Escoffier, a surgeon in Paris, had given the seventeenth-century house in which his grandfather was born to the municipality of Villeneuve-Loubet, which has leased it to us for ninety-nine years at an annual rent of one franc. We've engaged an architect to rebuild and enlarge it. We plan to make it the foremost gastronomical museum in the world."

"As soon as we succeed in resettling the five families who are still living in it," Mr. Philippe said.

"The museum will have the greatest library of cookbooks in the world, including manuscripts and incunabula, and also books on wine, and collections of wineglasses and historical wine labels,"

Mr. Donon said. "I'm giving it my collection of menus—of Escoffier Society dinners, among others. We have just rented a seventeenth-century mill near the Escoffier site; we plan to convert it into a restaurant attached to the museum. Then, right next to the Escoffier property, in the old Hotel Bellerive, we are going to open a culinary school, at which chefs will be trained in the Escoffier tradition. The school will recruit its faculty from retired chefs living on the French Riviera, where there are more of them to be found than in any other region in the world. The hotel has already been bought, and remodeling will begin soon, Philippe and I between us put up a hundred thousand dollars to cover the purchases and expenses."

"Donon has spent his time and money in a prodigal manner to promote French cooking," Mr. Philippe said.

"I have some letters at home from Mr. Frick," Mr. Donon began, but his co-founder, who had finished his steak, reminded him that they were due at a scholarship meeting of the Society's Foundation. Before the two Amis hurried away, I besought Mr. Donon to bring the letters, along with any other useful documentation he might have of his life and times, to our next lunch.

My next meeting with Mr. Donon also took place in the Gaucho Room, on a day, a couple of weeks later, when he was in town to conduct a wine-tasting session of the Comite de la Bonne Bouche of Les Amis d'Escoffier Society, at which the wines for the Diner d'Automne were to be selected. Mr. Donon, a reliable and cooperative man, had heeded my request for reference material, and after ordering smoked salmon, lamb chops, and a good Tavel he unrolled the Rhode Island poster. It bore the legend "First for Fishing. Rhode Island. America's First Vacationland," and showed the permanently vacationing *toque blance*, clad in dungarees, a lumberman's checked shirt, a sun visor, and high rubber boots, and almost knee-deep in the surf, holding up his big fish, a pleased smile on his face, and his rod resting on a rock behind him. "A neighbor saw me coming home with that fish on my back and called up a photographer," he said. "The photographer took a bunch of pictures, and one of them ended up on this poster, which the Rhode Island Development Council has circulated around the state to chambers of commerce, department stores, travel agencies, hotels, gasoline stations, and bait-and-tackle shops. It's displayed on the Jamestown-Newport ferries, too. My name isn't on it, as you can see, but ferry passengers sometimes recognize me and write me letters about it."

Going backward, chronologically, through his memorabilia, Rhode Island's silent barker next produced a copy of the menu of the five-chef Lobster Lafayette-christening dinner, on which the new baby was listed as "Le Homard 'Lafayette' dans sa Robe Roughe sur un Lit Perle"—translated, for the benefit of the partaking philanthropists, as "A Whole Baby Lobster in its Carapace on a Bed of Pearled Rice." He then handed me a congratulatory post-*homard* letter, on Knickerbocker Club stationery, from Mr. Crowninshield.

Mr. Donon thereupon pushed the calendar back twenty-seven years more—to 1914, when, only six months after his marriage, he returned to his homeland to serve as a sargeant with the French infantry in the First World War. By way of exhibit, he adduced a clipping from the Washington *Post* that read:

FRICK'S CHEF GOES TO WAR
High-Priced French Cook Leaves For Battlefield

Boston, August 7 – Inspired by patriotism of so high an order that he willingly gave up his highly paid position, the famous French chef employed by Henry Clay Frick at his North Shore summer home has resigned his place and announced his intention of returning to France to fight.

The consternation in the Frick family at this unexpected move, however, was duplicated in several other homes, where nearly all the man servants have either gone or have announced their intention of leaving.

The high-priced patriot, who has since become an American citizen, was severely wounded, and rendered unfit for further service, by a shellburst in February, 1916. Officially, he was invalided out—with the Croix de Guerre avec Palme as well as the Medaille Militarie – in January, 1917, but he actually returned to this country and, briefly, to Frick's employ in the summer of 1916. "I was almost crippled at first," he said, "but I was marvelously treated by Dr. Peter P. Johnson, then chief surgeon at the Beverly Hospital, in Beverly, near Prides Crossing. He made me a new left shoulder, grafted from my ribs. He refused to send me a bill. I still have thirty-two pieces of shrapnel in my left side – I feel them occasionally – and I have no left collar bone. When I'm fishing, this causes me to cast in a rather peculiar way, something like the twist."

The Frick household, I gathered, was not very well organized, causing Donon a good many ennuis in addition to his health, and a few months after his return to it he began, with Mr. Frick's blessing, to look elsewhere - - a bygone crisis that he made graphic for me with a flourish of photostatted documents, offering for my inspection a To Whom It May Concern letter, dated February 16, 1917, from his employer:

Joseph Donon was in our employ for three years as chef, and left to go to the war between France and Germany. He gave us entire satisfaction and we can highly recommend him.
H.C. Frick

Another, dated March 17th:

Joseph Donon
Dear Sir,

    I hear from Mr. Frick that you are looking for a position. Will you kindly meet me at 5 East 73rd St. on Monday morning next, the 19th, at 11:30 o'clock.

Truly,
Ruth Twombly

And a third, undated, but obviously written on the nineteenth or the twentieth:

Chef:

    Will you please come to 684 Fifth Avenue on Wednesday morning next, the 21st at 9:30 to see Mrs. Twombly.

Truly,
Ruth Twombly

"The East Seventy-third Street appointment, at which Miss Twombly interviewed me, was at the house of her sister, Mrs. Burden," he told me. "*'Mais vous etes trop jeune pour etre chef,'* she said, but she engaged me, anyway. I have one more letter here for you - - from Mr. Frick's secretary." Dated March 22nd, the day after Donon met Mrs. Twombly, this read:

Dear Mr. Donon:

    Mr. Frick is pleased you have gotten the position with Mrs. Twombly; it is probably the best position in New York. She does a great deal of entertainment, and you will of course have a great deal of work, which is all the better. Mr. Frick hopes you will make every effort to give entire satisfaction.

    The efforts that Mr. Donon proceeded to make, as he outlined them at our initial lunch, are a matter of culinary history. His salary with the Twomblys has been reported by a succession of

Cholly Knickerbockers and other students of the good life to have been twenty-five thousand dollars a year, with a house and living expenses thrown in—a report that he declined either to confirm or to deny. "To stress such salaries tends to arouse dissatisfaction in the working classes and make them dislike people like the Twomblys, who fulfilled a useful economic function in their day," he said. "They were considerate employers, and they gave work to a great many people. They were generous. In the end, they left me quite a nice sum—enough to live on, apart from my U.S. Steel stock. My wife and I used to go to France every second or third summer – summers when the Twomblys also went abroad—and Mrs. Twombly made me a present of those trips. She was democratic. She was like a mother to me. During the last two years of her life, she had three nurses and was on a diet. Soufflés, mostly (I'd vary these: spinach, chicken, liver, and so forth), and vegetables and fruit. The day before she died, she ate a chicken soufflé."

"How old was she when she died?" I asked.

"Ninety-eight," Mr. Donon said. "Almost ninety-nine. I think her daughter's relieving her of most of her responsibilities contributed to her long life."

Mr. Philippe, who had again been invited to lunch with us, now arrived, twenty-five minutes late, and accompanied by Robert Huyot, the general manager of the Summit.

"I must confess that the *perdreau* at the last Lucullus Circle dinner was disappointing," Mr. Huyot said, with an admirable lack of chauvinism, since this dining-club feast had taken place at his own hotel, where the object of his criticism had been listed on the menu as "Le Perdreau Roti sur Canape a la Facon du Summit." "It was not the chef's fault; some of the birds were tough. If you serve partridge, they must all be of the same hatch. Otherwise, sometimes one will be good but another may be tough."

"I used to buy partridge through Arsene Tingaud, on Second Avenue," Mr. Donon said. "Today, people buy meat at chain stores, where the quality is uneven. If you buy from a butcher who knows you, like Tingaud, you get the best."

Mr. Donon expressed a hope that Philippe and Huyot would grace the Bonne Bouche tasting later that afternoon, and he also invited me to attend, *in statu pupillari*. Following an after-lunch siesta, I accordingly showed up at a suite in the Biltmore where a dozen men were sitting around a table decorated with ferns, candlesticks, cheese, and crackers. As I joined them, Mr. Donon began distributing copies of a printed menu of the forthcoming Diner d'Autonine, to which a score card was appended, to wit:

White Burgundy	1	2	2-A
Red Burgundy	3	4	4-A
Bordeaux		5	6

"Each wine under consideration has a number," he explained, for my benefit. "Candidates are sent in by various dealers, and from these we have selected eight, from which three will be chosen, one in each category. Taste must be the only criterion, since the wines are identified solely by number and we won't see the bottles until a decision is reached. The Comite de la Bonne Bouche has about fifty members, but, of course, not all of them appear at any given meeting."

"Please vote only for your first choice in each class," said Vincent J. Coyle, president of Les Amis d'Escoffier Society and managing director of Essex House. "Just make a ring around your choice."

Two waiters, working out of an adjoining pantry, passed trays of half-filled glasses of white wine – Candidate No. 1, to go with the autumnal fish, supreme de Turbotin a la Bonne-Femme.

"Take your time," Mr. Donon said, as all sipped in silence. "The Comite de la Bonne Bouche is on the spot now."

No. 1 was succeeded by No. 2, and then No. 2 by No. 2-A.

The man at my right, Harold P. Bock, general manager of the Sheraton-East Hotel, pointed to his second glass.

"That's right," said the man at my left, Michel L. Dreyfus, of Dreyfus, Ashby & Co., dealers in wines and spirits. "*Le premier est trop sec.*"

"The bouquet of that second is terrific," said another juryman, whom Mr. Donon had introduced to me as Frank G. Cummiskey, a commissioner of the Workmen's Compensation Board of the State of New York.

"If you're ready, mark your choices and we'll take your glasses away," Mr. Donon said.

Each committeeman drew a circle around the number of his preference, and Mr. Donon invited me to do likewise, as an *amicus curiae*, but I feared this might throw the whole Diner out of focus, so I stayed my hand.

At intervals, in came trays of the three red Burgundies, one of which would be privileged to wash down Le Perdreau Pocle a la Perigourdine.

"The partridge will be served with a rather rich sauce," Mr. Donon said. "It needs a pretty good wine, you know."

No one seemed to like No. 3. "This is a tough choice—these two," said William R. Ebersol, general manager of the Hotel Pierre, indicating Nos. 4 and 4-A.

"Both so good I can hardly make up my mind," said Mr. Donon, beaming.

"It's going to be a close vote," Mr. Bock said to me. "I favor Four-A, to cut the sauce. Four is too soft."

"Number Five, gentlemen," Mr. Donon said as the first of the two Bordeaux was passed. "We're now with the cheese, as you know. At our last session, we had a tie on the Bordeaux. What a battle that was!"

Presently, the ballots were collected and examined by Donon and Coyle. No. 6 and No. 4 won; Nos. 2 and 2-A were tied.

"I'll change my vote to Two," someone said, and a battle was averted.

The competing bottles were produced and the winners revealed as Meursault Perriers '59, Chambertin Clos de Beze '55, and Chateau Haut-Brion '55.

In due course, I attended the Diner d'Automne, as Mr. Donon's guest, and not long afterward, by way of fractional reciprocity, on a Friday when he came down from Villa Chez-Nous to attend a meeting of L'Academie Culinaire de France, I took him to lunch at the San Marino Restaurant, on East Fifty-third Street, whose cooking I admire. "As it happens," he said after we had agreed on a choice of Ravioli San Marino, bay scallops, watercress salad, and a bottle of Tavel, "I'm also in town to pick up a dozen terrapin, on Front Street, for a luncheon for twenty-four that Mr. Burden is giving for his mother at the Pavillon next Wednesday, which is her eightieth birthday. 'You'll have to make one dish for her,' he said. 'Terrapin a la Florham.' Well, I haven't been in business for six or seven years, but I made Terrapin a la Florham for Mrs. Burden on her visits to Florham for twenty-eight years – ever since I originated it, in 1926—and I couldn't refuse. We used to serve it twice a week in season. You need one terrapin of three to four pounds for two portions – I use only the black meat, not the white—and plenty of eggs. It takes three days to clean and cook the terrapin. I'll take them—alive, of course—to Rhode Island in my car tomorrow morning, prepare them at home, bring them down to the Pavillon Wednesday morning, and finish them up there in forty-five minutes. I've arranged that with my friend Henri Soule and with the Pavillon's chef, Clement Grangier. It's unusual for one chef to let another come in and use his kitchen. I've asked Mr. Burden precisely when he wants them served. One-fifteen."

We started on our ravioli, and I asked just what it was that constituted the Florham aspect of Florham terrapin.

"It's the way it's finished—the sauce," Mr. Donon said. "It's between the Maryland style and the Philadelphia style. The Maryland has a brown sauce; the Philadelphia sauce is yellow-white. I make a blending of the two by adjusting the amount of egg yolk, beaten with cream, that is added to the other ingredients. Less eggs and cream than in the Philadelphia, more than in the Maryland. Properly cooked, it takes a lot of work, but really, I will say, it's good. It's delicious."

Mr. Donon took a sip of Travel and, at my suggestion, described the Academie Culinaire. "The parent organization is in Paris," he said, "and there are chapters in Dijon and New York. Each group is limited to twenty-four members—all chefs with at least twenty-five years of professional experience. We meet three or four times a year to look over new recipes—today's meeting is at the Essex House—and we give annual dinners among chefs, with occasional outside guests.

Terrapin à la Florham

4 terrapins, 3 1/2 pounds each
2 cups dry sherry
1 tablespoon crushed black peppercorns
1 pound sweet butter
3 egg yolks
1/2 cup heavy cream

Drop the terrapin in tepid water and allow it to swim for 30 minutes. Wash it well and plunge it into boiling water, which will kill it quickly and painlessly. Remove the thin white skin from the feet and tail with a rough cloth. Cut off the claws and draw out the head with a skewer or steel needle. Plunge the head into boiling water to loosen the skin, and rub the skin off.

Put the prepared terrapin in a kettle and cover it with cold water. Add no salt or other seasoning. Bring the water to a boil, cover the kettle, and cook until the terrapin is tender. This takes from 30 minutes to an hour or more: the terrapin is tender when the paws feel soft to the pressure of the finger. Cool the terrapin in the kettle, uncovered, overnight.

To remove the meat, lay the terrapin on its back. Detach the meat from the shells with the top of a small knife. Break the shell on the flat side and remove the legs, the neck, and the head. Separate the liver and eggs from the entrails. Be careful not to break the gall bladder, which is attached to the liver, as the gall will give a bitter flavor to everything it touches. If the gall bladder should break, wash the meat very carefully in running cold water.

Discard the white meat and the intestines, which are inedible. Use the dark meat, the fat, the liver, and the eggs. Clean and slice the liver and soak it in cold water. Soak the eggs in cold water; the skin should be removed before the eggs are used. Cut the dark meat into pieces the size of a walnut, put it into a bowl, and cover with a wet towel.

Remove the skin from the lower shell and break the shell into pieces. Return the shell and the bones removed from the terrapin to the liquid in which it was cooked. Cook for 10 minutes, strain the broth, and reduce it over low heat, skimming from time to time, until there is just enough clear, light brown stock to cover the terrapin meat in the bowl. This stock is highly gelatinous, and has a strong but pleasant flavor. Store the terrapin in the refrigerator.

Put the jellied terrapin, prepared as above, in a heavy-bottomed pan and melt it very slowly. Heat 1 cup of sherry in a small saucepan with the pepper, stirring constantly, and strain the boiling wine into the terrapin. Add a little salt and cook for 2 minutes. Fit a flannel cloth over a large bowl and put a colander on the cloth. Pour the terrapin and its juices into the colander. Remove the *colander and set it, covered, in a warm place. Strain the juices through the cloth and return them to a saucepan. Reduce over high heat, skimming as necessary, until the juices are thick and syrupy.*

Watch carefully during this process to prevent burning. Add the terrapin to the reduced sauce and swirl in the butter, bit by bit. Heat the remaining cup of sherry and add it to the pan. Adjust the seasoning with salt. If desired, the flavor of the sauce may be modified and the color lightened by the addition of the egg yolks beaten with the cream: this is the Maryland style.

Remove the skin from the terrapin eggs, plunge them into boiling water for a moment, and sprinkle them over the prepared terrapin. The terrapin may be kept hot for serving in a chafing dish. Serves 8.

———————

We cover the provinces of France with our cookery; each dinner reflects the style of a different province. Last year's was devoted to Alsace; this year's, in April, will be Provence, in honor of Escoffier. At that dinner, as an innovation, we will name a Chef of the Year—the man who has done the most to promote French cuisine in America during the preceding year. His name will be engraved on a silver cup, which he will keep for a year and then turn over to the next year's champion. It's the same idea as the Davis Cup in tennis. Our choice as the first Chef of the Year has already been made—Raymond Grangier, the brother of the Grangier at the Pavillon, the chef of the France, the new French liner. Our academy operates something like the French Academy; a new member is elected only when death creates a vacancy. All the chairs are named after famous chefs, and the new member delivers a speech on the man for whom his chair is named. I succeeded to the New York chapter's chair of Escoffier."

"What did you say about him?" I asked.

"Well, it was ten years ago, and I don't recall exactly," Mr. Donon replied. "But today I would say this: At the beginning of Escoffier's career, cooking, as a profession, was not held in high esteem, owing partly to the laxity that had crept into so many kitchens and partly to the rigorous conditions of kitchen work—oppressive heat, and so on. He fought that slackness and improved those conditions—at both the Savoy and the Carlton in London—and his example was widely followed. He originated new methods of cooking to fit a post-Edwardian period in which leisurely dining was modified by a time element—methods stressing simplicity with no sacrifice of quality—and as a result the best French cooking is not very complicated. Escoffier's methods are reflected in his great 'Guide Culinaire.' His taste was impeccable. He neither drank nor smoked. He was a great believer in the virtue of remaining calm. He was a diminutive figure, very lively, precise in his movements, with small, skillful hands. He lived for his trade."

The scallops were served, and Mr. Donon pronounced them excellent.

Chef Donon and Les Amis d'Escoffier Society

During his years as chef to the Twomblys and after the deaths of Florence and Ruth Twombly, Joseph Donon played a central role in world cuisine, especially in the United States and France. Having served as a student of Auguste Escoffier in his youth, he founded the Les Amis d'Escoffier Society with several other chefs in 1936, serving as president until his retirement. Donon also founded and was president of the Auguste Escoffier Foundation Museum of Villeneuve-Loubet, Alpes Maritimes, Provence.

In addition, Chef Donon was one of the six founders of the American Academy of Chefs, serving as secretary general for 25 years, as well as editor of Culinary Review and the author of a number of cookbooks. The Academy sponsored the Escoffier Society.

Beyond his many activities in the culinary world, he was a member and president of the Les Medailles Militaires de New York, a branch of the Paris-centered association of war veterans who have been decorated with France's highest honor, and which raises funds for the orphans of other veterans.

When Donon was fifteen and was an assistant to the chef in the household of the Marquis de Penise-Passy, at Villeneuve-Loubet, Escoffier's birthplace, the Marquis introduced him to Escoffier. Escoffier invited Donon to work for him at the Carlton, in London, and he became a protégée of the most significant chef of his time. Later in life Donon wrote a brief reflection on his time with Escoffier and the man himself:

Musée de l'art culinaire

ESCOFFIER'S ACHIEVEMENTS

by Joesph Donon

At the beginning of Escoffier's career, cooking was not a profession held in high esteem. This was partly due to the laxity which could so easily creep in and also to the rigorous conditions of kitchen work. A cook spends the greater part of his time around the stove in oppressing heat. Escoffier was quick to realize these conditions, the cuisine suffered, the atmosphere in the kitchen suffered even more. He, with this small stature, was destined to suffer even more than others from the heat of the stoves. As an example to others he never allowed himself to drink or smoke. He made it a point of honor to preserve his impeccable taste. He was a great believer in the virtue of remaining calm.

Escoffier carried to their most logical ends the reforms which he was introducing into the whole field of culinary art. He was concerned too with his employees' educational status and advised them to acquire the culture which their professional training, often begun at an early age, had prevented them from attaining. The life of Escoffier was one of simplicity and hard work, ever doing and studying new formulas, adding to the knowledge of cookery, consecrating his efforts to bring the public to a finer appreciation of the art of cooking and eating. To him the art of cooking depended upon the psychology of the public; it followed the impulses they manifested where life is easy and without too much preoccupation. The art of cooking follows a line of leisurely dining, but when a time element is involved, Escoffier felt that cooking had to be adopted to the situation.

We see Escoffier laboring to this end and simplifying the method of cooking. This he did without sacrificing the quality that distinguishes classical cooking. Among his books, "Le Guide Culinaire" or "A Guide to Modern Cookery" marks the inauguration of an entirely new style of living. His motto was that no matter what changes take place, cooking will always be one of the most agreeable pleasures given to human beings, and that to make it so is a trust placed upon the chef. Escoffier enjoyed his early triumphs in the glamorous cosmopolitan hotels of Europe, and his career's fulfillment in the fantastic Edwardian years in London at The Savoy and The Carlton when he reigned as the supreme exponent of gastronomic excellence. Amidst these scenes of splendor, the diminutive figure of this great artist moved with quiet dignity. A slave to duty, utterly unspoiled by adulation, devoting his working hours to devising new culinary masterpieces and his scanty leisure to unheralded acts of benevolence.

It was my good fortune to complete my training as a chef under Maitre Escoffier during his Carlton Hotel days, and to be one of the many hundreds of chefs he sent over to America. For the last 26 years it has been my privilege to be one of the Friends of Escoffier Societies who are dedicated to the propagation of the high standards and ethics of the culinary profession thus perpetuating the memory of the great culinary master, Auguste Escoffier.

THE ESCOFFIER SOCIETY

Jack Alexander, writing in *The New Yorker* of March 20, 1937 when Les Amis d'Escoffier was very new, reported that at the time its membership was limited to one hunded, of which sixty percent were chefs, maitres d'hotels, wine stewards, and restaurateurs. He wrote that of all the dozen of so gourmet societies in New York Les Amis is "the most fussy and fastidious," arranging its dinners "with the formality of seconds arranging for a duel." Every important New York chef in the 1930s had studied with Escoffier in his kitchen.

Participants submit menus to be judged by a four-man committee, for which Joseph Donon was a special advisor. The main dish had to be an invention of Auguste Escoffier, with the privilege for the entrant of proposing one dish of his own invention. "Let your creation please," Alexander writes, "and you will bask n the warmth of expert approval. Let your sauces disappoint these precisians, or our soup fall a shade short of perfection, and you will suffer a loss of face comparable to that of a surgeon who bungles an operation before the Academy."

The Society today is much less forboding, with a vision "To continue the standards of haute cuisine and culinary tradition established by Auguste Escoffier by marrying the resources of respected culinary professionals and enthusiasts in the sharing of common culinary experiences, and also recognizing achievement in, and providing support of, culinary education through scholarships for students."

It gathers monthly for dinners dedicated to perfecting the art of fine dining, with a goal of making these dinners an educational experience for amateurs and professionals alike. Food is assessed by leading food and wine professionals for its preparation, texture, presentation and service.

Les Amis d'Escoffier Society
OF NEW YORK INC.
(FRIENDS OF ESCOFFIER)

Les Amis d'Escoffier Society Foundation, Inc.
(FRIENDS OF ESCOFFIER)
349 WEST 48TH STREET
NEW YORK 36. N. Y.

Maître Escoffier

Auguste Escoffier was born in Villeneuve-Loubet, Alpes Maritimes, France on October 28th, 1846. On February 12th, 1935, a few days after the death of his wife, Escoffier died at his home, La Villa Fernand, 8 bis Avenue de la Costa, Monte Carlo, in his eighty-ninth year. His remains are buried in the family vault at Villeneuve-Loubet.

La bonne cuisine est la base du véritable bonheur

A. Escoffier

Mai 1911

BROILED DEVILED CHICKEN

One 3-pound chicken
Dry mustard
1/2-cup bread crumbs
4 tablespoons butter
2 tablespoons chopped parsley, chives, tarragon
2 garlic cloves juice of one lemon

1 *Have the chicken split in half, remove all the bones, except for the lower part of the leg.*

2. *Season with salt and pepper.*

3. *Make a paste of the dry mustard, with it brush the chicken on both sides. Sprinkle both sides with bread crumbs. Sprinkle with the melted butter and broil on a baking pan in a moderate oven, 350 degrees for 15 to 20 minutes on both sides.*

4. *Remove the chicken to a platter, and add to the pan juices, the herbs and lemon juice. Adjust the seasoning, and pour it over the chicken on the platter.*

COEUR A LA CREME
(CHEESE HEART)

2 cups cottage cheese
2 cups cream cheese
2 cups heavy cream

Force the cheese through a very fine sieve and beat it well with a rotary beater. Whip the cream stiff and stir it into the cheese. Line a heart-shaped basket mold with cheese cloth, and turn the cheese mixture into it. Put the mold on a plate and let it stand overnight in the refrigerator. To serve, unmold the heart on a chilled serving dish and pour some light cream over it. Surround the heart with chilled strawberries sweetened to taste.

GOURGERE BOURGUINGNONNE
(CHEESE PUFFS)

1 cup milk
1/3-cup butter
1/4-teaspoon salt
7/8-cup of flour
4 eggs
1 cup Swiss cheese, diced

1. *In a thick flat-bottomed saucepan, bring the milk, butter and salt to a boil.*
2. *Remove the pan from the heat, mix in the flour with a wooden spoon, and then dry the dough over a slow fire, stirring constantly until it comes away easily from the sides of the pan. Remove the pan from the stove and mix in the eggs, one at a time. Then blend in the diced cheese.*

Puffs
1. *With a tablespoon scoop out pieces of dough on a baking sheet, each the size of a small egg.*
2. *Bake in the oven at 325 degrees. It takes about 35 to 40 minutes.*
3. *Serve hot or cold*

Note: The puffs can be scooped up with a pastry bag. The size of the baking sheet should be 18-by-14 inches and heavy. It is wise to add another baking sheet underneath when cooking to prevent burning.

JOSEPH DONON'S FINAL YEARS

Chef Donon enjoyed his time as a member of the Newport community until his death at age 93 on March 20, 1982. He could see the water from his home, "Chez Nous," to Newport and the mansions where the wealthy enjoyed his unique French cuisine, especially Vinland, the summer home of Florence Vanderbilt Twombly, where he spent many summers as the head chef.

In addition to gardening, one of his favorite pastimes was surfcasting. Each morning at three o'clock a.m. from June to October, he would drive to the ocean and spend the morning salt-water fishing. In 1958 he caught a huge striped bass, a fish fifty-four inches long and thirty-two inches in girth. The photograph of Donon and the bass almost his size was featured on a poster to attract tourists.

On Nov. 16, 1981, the New England Chapter of the Les Amis d'Escoffier Society honored Joseph Donon at its annual dinner with an honorary membership in the Honorary Order of the Golden Toque. Joseph Donon died five months later. The funeral was private, and his burial was in France.

Joseph Donon at 90 with his cocker spaniel Charbonnette

The Famille Blaudin-Donon grave

ABOUT THE AUTHORS

Walter Cummins, a professor of English emeritus at Fairleigh Dickinson University, with graduate degrees from the University of Iowa, has published seven short story collections and stories, essays, articles, and reviews in many magazines. An Honorary Trustee of the Friends of Florham, he is one of the authors of *Florham: The Lives of an American Estate* and *Florham: An American Treasure*.

Arthur T. Vanderbilt II, a graduate of Wesleyan University and the University of Virginia School of Law, is the author of many books of history, biography, memoirs, and essays. He became fascinated with Florham while researching and writing his book *Fortune's Children: The Fall of the House of Vanderbilt*. He is an Honorary Trustee of the Friends of Florham and has written many articles for the Friends of Florham publication. He wrote an introduction for *Florham: The Lives of an American Estate*, and is one of the authors of *Florham: An American Treasure*.

Our special thanks to Robert DeLage, a long-time friend of Joseph Donon, for making available the Donon memoir, the Donon photographs and memorabilia, and his invaluable advice, without which this book would not have been possible.

november 21-1981

Thank
You

for everything. Joseph Dowoy

CPSIA information can be obtained
at www.ICGtesting.com
Printed in the USA
LVHW071704250219
608675LV00001B/1/P

9 780692 893371